So, You Want to Buy a Shelter…

Your Guide to Planning
A Soft Covered Structure Purchase

Published by CreateSpace and in association with My Inspired Communications
Copyright ©2018 by Norman Eygenraam, Multi Shelter Solutions
Palmerston, Ontario, Canada
First Edition, 2018

Disclaimer
This book is meant as a guide to help inform the reader of all the choices and options to consider as they prepare to purchase a structure. Since Norman has been in the Greenhouse business 45 years and selling them for more than half that time, the references made in this guide are to the ones he has had experience with, and which Multi Shelter Solutions currently sells. Norman and Multi Shelter Solutions are not responsible in any way for the choices the reader makes due to the advice written in this book. The planning decisions are the sole responsibility of the reader and this book is meant as a guide only, written from personal experience.

The publisher does not have control over and does not assume responsibility for the author or third party websites. The publisher nor the author shall be liable for any physical, psychological, emotional, financial, or commercial damages, including but not limited to special, incidental, consequential or other damages.
So, You Want to Buy a Structure may be purchased for educational, business or promotional purposes
Permission should be addressed in writing to multisheltersales@gmail.com or Multi Shelter Solutions PO Box 1125 Palmerston, ON N0G2P0

Cover and Interior Design by:
Andrea Eygenraam, My Inspired Communications

ISBN-13: 978-1717105868

ISBN-10: 1717105866

ACKNOWLEDGEMENTS

A special thank you to the all the customers over the years who have helped Norm gain the knowledge that he is sharing in this book

We wish to thank our team in the office and at the shop who help keep things running smoothly each day: Gwen, Carson, Terry, Doug, & Jeff

Norm wishes to thank Heather for her support.

Norm wishes to thank Andrea for coming up with the idea and bringing this project to life.

And especially we want to thank YOU for picking this book and we wish you the best of luck in your structure journey!

A Typical Multi Shelter Structure

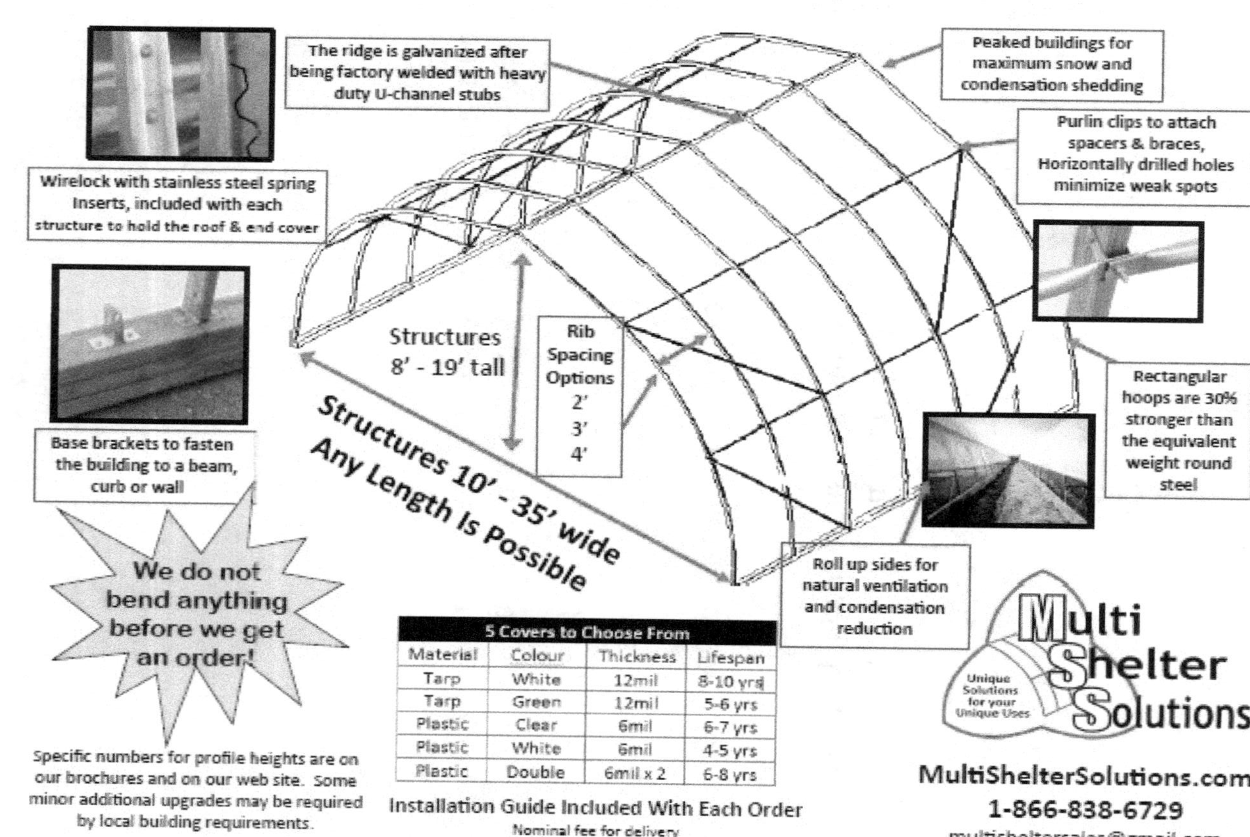

5 Covers to Choose From			
Material	Colour	Thickness	Lifespan
Tarp	White	12mil	8-10 yrs
Tarp	Green	12mil	5-6 yrs
Plastic	Clear	6mil	6-7 yrs
Plastic	White	6mil	4-5 yrs
Plastic	Double	6mil x 2	6-8 yrs

FOREWORD

This book is meant as a guide to help inform you of all the choices and options to consider as you prepare to purchase a structure. Please note, many times in this book a particular point may be touched on briefly, and then later covered in greater detail.

You will find small grey squares like the one above, throughout this book. Over the years there is not much Norm hasn't seen, and we have included some feature stories of his experiences throughout this book to help illustrate some key points.

Since Norm has been in the Greenhouse business 45 years and selling them for more than half that time, please keep in mind, the references made in this guide are to the ones he has had experience with, and which Multi Shelter Solutions currently sells, as that is what we are able to reference the easiest.

We have tried to make this book as informative as possible, no matter which direction you choose to go.

As always, please don't hesitate to contact us if you have any questions.

TABLE OF CONTENTS

GLOSSARY

Anchor Post: a steel tube which is pounded into ground to directly anchor the building. The top part is partially flattened to fit inside the hoop. (see photo 1)

Base Bracket: is a formed strip of steel that uses lag bolts to secure it to the base beam. The hoop slides over top for fastening and stability. (see photo 2)

Cathedral: a shape of structure installed with the long straight side down to allow greater height when less floor space is required

Cross-tie: It is the same material as wind brace except longer. It is used to tie the left and right side of the structure together for strength and stability.

Gothic: a shape of structure that is rounded at the base and goes up to a peak.

Hoops: also called **arch or rib**, is the curved piece of rectangular tubing making up the primary framework or skeleton of the structure, either 1"x2" or 1"x3"

Inflator Fan: small fan that blows air continuously to maintain an air space between two layers of plastic (see photo 3)

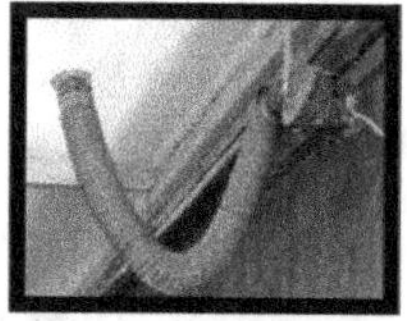

Pipe strap: a steel bracket fitting around the hoop used to attach wood or steel beams to the structure. A lighter & wider version of the base bracket (photo 1)

Plastic: is a covering for structures which can be done in single or double layer. MSS standard is 6mil and can come in either white or clear.

Purlin: horizontal bar (shorter than a wind brace) used for spacing and structural support between the hoops. Both ends are flattened and have a hole.

Purlin Clip: a "U" shaped bracket to attach purlins or wind braces to hoop (photo 4)

Ridge: or spine of the structure with factory welded stubs that are used to secure the top end of the hoop.

Ridge Connector: 8" piece of "U" Channel used to join 2 sections of ridge

Ridge Cross/Starter: a piece of ridge with a pair of stubs at each end, comes preinstalled into the first ridge piece (see photo 5)

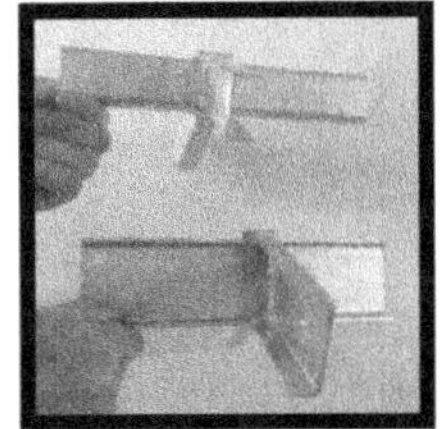

Ridge Stub: an angle cut u-channel which is welded to the ridge steel tube. It goes into the top end of the hoop. (diagonal pieces on photo 5)

Roll up sidewall: a mechanism to allow the full-length cover of the structure to be opened up. Usually both sides have the capacity for roll up (see photo 6)

Sill Plate: usually a double 2x6 or 2x8 placed on top of the posts, it bridges the gap between the posts or ties the base beams together. In the case of a railroad tie, it also gives consistency to the top surface to allow level construction of the building

Tarp: is a woven form of plastic which has much greater tear resistance. MSS standard is 12mil and can come in either white or green.

Wind Brace: similar tube to a purlin (although longer) and installed diagonally at each corner of the structure. The quantity per corner depends on the structure.

Wirelock Channel: an aluminum channel generally installed on the first and last hoop where cover is inserted. It can also be used at the top and/or bottom of the rollup. (see photo 7, left)

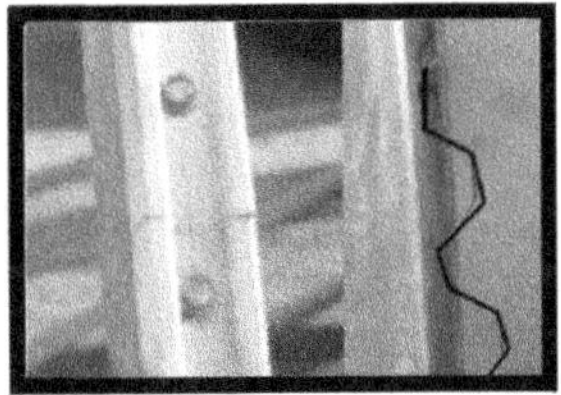

Wirelock Insert: the "zip-zag" stainless, heat-treated steel wire used in the wirelock channel to hold the covering in place (see photo 7, right)

PART ONE:
YOUR STRUCTURE

CHAPTER ONE:
KNOWING THE BASICS BEFORE YOU BUY

KEY TAKEAWAY: Make Your Educated Wish List, Balance all considerations

Knowing the basics when you are starting the process of purchasing a shelter includes having a firm handle on:

What You are Trying to Accomplish and **What You are Dealing with**.

This applies for both greenhouses and storage structures. By efficiently choosing from all of the structure choices in combination with your goals and the restrictions or challenges in the best possible way, you will be creating a structure package that is going to serve you well for years to come.

You might be wondering……

- What is a structure? Why is it necessary?

- What are some of my choices and the consequences of my choices?

- Structure choices are determined by purpose, size, shape, covering, orientation and location. How do you prioritize?

A structure is simply a covered frame that protects our items from the elements or fading. Simply adding different types of covers, now greenhouses can also become extremely economical shelters.

Using white plastic or tarp for livestock is an economical housing solution to provide shade, while still being able to reduce condensation and temperature fluctuations with a double plastic cover similar to a greenhouse.

Covering equipment with a tarp building provides protection for valuables as well as reducing fading from the sun or damage from the elements.

FOR YOUR WISH LIST

Make your wish list. Prioritize your wish list. Research the options for your wish list. Ask questions. Reprioritize your wish list. Repeat.

The first place you must start with is **your goal or purpose**. There is quite a bit of conflicting information out there and without a very detailed plan and focus for your project, you can easily get off the rails.

Your goals will need to be specifically spelled out and will likely be modified once the realities of some of the obstacles have been determined.

> **Goals should always include both short and long-term plans since some structures and layouts are easier to expand then others.**

Making a wish list of the things you are dealing with and the things you would like the building to do can be a good start.

> What can you change or not change?

If your plans and goals include an aggressive expansion plan, it is more important than ever to get off on the right foot and start in the right direction. It would be best to address those issues NOW, BEFORE you have a complicated and expensive hole to get yourself out of. It is a lot cheaper and easier to go back to the drawing board before you have the posts in the ground.

Restrictions or challenges are not just limited to wind, snow load and other climatic issues.

Accessibility of water, power, roadways, building codes and market opportunities could also impact where and what you can or should build.

> As each of these parts are researched and developed, they will be impacted by the reality of your budget. By knowing your options, you will be able to get best value for your investment

Another point regarding your goals and purpose is to **be flexible**. Your life may not go according to your plans. If you do not build flexibility into your project, it will get very expensive to change it.

WHAT ARE YOU DEALING WITH?

This list includes things that you see as challenges to achieving your goals

The **climate** is much more brutal in Thunder Bay than Leamington. The **snowfall** is much bigger in Barrie than in Dundas. It is a lot **windier** in Shelburne than in Caledon, even though they are neighbours. There are a lot less **rocks** and **hills** in Dresden than Kingston.

Maybe you have a rookie banker who is determined to eliminate all risk. Maybe you are stuck on a postage stamp size lot. The list can go on and on.

A very important consideration for your structure is how it **handles the weather**. Structures can be beefed up to make them better at **snow shedding** or **wind deflection** and altered so they are more **heat efficient** for both saving it in the winter and expelling it in the summer.

Structure choices include not only **size** and **profile** but many choices of **coverings**. **Anchoring** choices will be determined by soil conditions and the possibility of relocating the building. **Ventilation** requirements will impact which structure package you choose. **Size, spacing and shape** of the hoops will allow you to effectively deal with the weather in your location.

> Many times over the years I have found potential customers trying to make their situation and requirements fit into a "preconceived box". A phrase that has been used many times is "Tell me what you need and leave the imagination up to me". I don't think there is an example of something that we have not "been there, done that!"

GETTING STARTED WITH YOUR SHELTER CUSTOMIZATION

There are many factors to consider when purchasing a structure. More so today then ever before, it is critical to speak with an experienced professional who knows the various challenges or pitfalls to be aware of and will work together with you to find a solution strategy for your specific requirements.

There are many choices for shapes, styles and sizes of structures. These choices, more than any other, will force you to strike a balance between strength and cost or return and cost.

There are many variables that will affect the cost per square foot of your building. Only by careful research and evaluation will you determine if a particular choice is a valid consideration for your application.

It is important to find the intersection points of

- what you would like to accomplish
- the location
- landscape
- climate circumstances you are faced with
- price range to be considered.

The following is a checklist we made up to help make sure you have all critical points covered and considered. Each one will be detailed more as we go along in this book.

1. **Pick a Location:** Your building **must** be level from side to side. If you can't excavate, we can design a variation. End to end slope is ok but if it is more than 1%, we need to know. If you are butting against a building, there may need to be some extra hoops in the first 12' of length. Building behind something does not provide shelter. This actually increases wind turbulence. These buildings aren't meant to go somewhere "that isn't good for anything else". We will address in more detail how to deal with not being level from side to side in the next chapter.

2. **Pick a width:** As you go wider, you need exponentially more steel and bracing which may or may not impact the ability to get engineered drawings.

Generally speaking, when you go wider, the top will be lowered, unless you go to longer lengths of steel. The opposite is true for going narrower.

3. Pick a length: Any length is possible; simply by adding hoops If you are building between 2 fixed points, the last hoop spacing can be modified to fit the spot.

4. Pick a height: Building higher will improve the **snow shedding** characteristics of the building. Building higher gives more interior space close to the wall but the structure catches more wind. Since building higher catches more wind, the structure may require reduced hoop spacing. Building higher will be a little costlier to heat but does improve natural air circulation. Building lower will decrease snow shedding and may require closer hoop spacing.

5. Pick a base or foundation: Base Brackets fasten under each hoop to secure the building to a beam. This beam can be ground mounted or on blocks, posts, slab or shipping containers.

Another option is a **welded steel base rail** if the structure needs to be moveable.

The last option is **Anchor Posts**. Each hoop would sit on a post that may need to be set into concrete. These hollow steel tubes are 1 ¼ "x 36" or 1 ¾ x 40". There is one anchor post per hoop, usually set into concrete. Anchor posts are not advisable for very heavy or stony ground because of shifting.

Anchoring the foundation is critical to the long-term life of the building. **Please remember that there simply is no such thing as too many anchors.**

6. **Pick a cover:** While considering your structure choices you will have to weigh cost versus benefit or return. There is no area which this is truer then with cover choices. The wide range of cover choices mainly include polyethylene and woven products, and many more. Within each of these products there is an equally great variety

of choices. Along with each of these choices there is a huge variation in cost and function or performance.

Doubling up on plastic reduces heat loss by 30%, minimizes condensation and increases life span by 50%. Packages with double cover include an inflator fan. This kit includes hanger bracket with adaptor to fasten to the inside layer of the cover. It is very effective for stiffening buildings in severely windy areas

7. Determine ventilation: Roll up Side Walls are an economical add on to our greenhouses or livestock shelters to provide natural ventilation. They have also been used for shop applications when you would be working in the structure during the hot summer months.

- No electricity needed with simple hand crank & stop

- Variable height possibilities according to wind area

- Roll up sides work best in combination with end vents located near the peak

Roof vents and **exhaust fans** are also available options

8. Building ends: There is a very large variety of options for ends that you will need to assess your needs in terms of doors, windows, and other openings. We do not recommend having one end open and one end closed as you will likely have an expensive kite.

ORGANIC GREENHOUSES AND BUILDINGS

There are many benefits to having a structure for organic growing and housing. Even though we discuss greenhouses, the concepts apply to all soft covered shelters.

They are often used a season extender for protecting crops from the elements, blight, and fungus. Since Organic growers and farmers do not use pesticides, this type of protection is often required for some of the more sensitive crops.

The structures are easy to move to allow the expansion of the growing area. These structures can easily help to give you the opportunity to grow more crops in a limited area.

What many of our customers also do, particularly with our movable and Hanley Tunnel structures (pictured above), is start growing the early crops under the protection of the structure, and as the crop is stable enough, they move the structure to be able to start the next planting.

Our structures are also used for organic livestock raising to ensure the animals have a healthy, safe and protected environment out of the elements.

They are versatile structures, and only require the changing of clear to white plastic for the various uses. The environment allows the animals to have sunlight, but still get the shade they require.

The combination of the **double layer of plastic**, **roll up sides**, and **inflator fan**, on both the greenhouse and livestock shelters, helps to **reduce condensation** and keep the structure **ventilated**.

18

We have researched a solar powered fan option, as well as a powerless alternative, for those off grid customers or if the structure is out in the field away from electricity as we know many of our organic growers and farmers are in these situations. These options are detailed further along in the book.

I have done three consecutive presentations at the local organic conference, Greenhouses 101, 202 and 303, each getting progressively more advanced. Since I have an extensive history in the industry and willingness to share this knowledge, and the organizer saw potential benefit to include me as a key speaker in 2015, 2016 and 2017. Videos of these presentations are available on our YouTube channel if you'd like more detailed information on these topics. Much of the information applies to soft covered structures as well in regards to lift, surviving the elements and other factors.

CHAPTER TWO:
PREPARATION AND OVERVIEW

KEY TAKEAWAY: Balance optimism of future plans with practical considerations of the present

LOCATION

Pick a Location: Your building **must** be level from side to side. If you can't excavate, a variation will be required. End to end slope is ok but if it is more than 1%, this needs to be addressed. If you are butting against a building, there may need to be some extra hoops in the first 12' of length. Building behind something does not provide shelter. You actually increase wind turbulence.

> So often the temptation is to put a building in a spot "that isn't good for anything else", but this is not recommended! Especially if this area is prone to excessive ground moisture, it will be a continuing problem as long as you have the building there.

When your location is not level from side to side, and levelling is challenging, there are ways of modifying the base or structure. We go into more detail on this online and encourage you to contact us for more information if this is your situation.

The location and orientation of a structure are two different things that need to be given careful thought to since the consequences are so long lasting.

> **Location** is more about **what <u>you</u> need** and **orientation** has to do with **what the <u>structure</u> needs to perform well.**

The cost of making changes after the fact are significant and often make it impossible.

- **Location** has to do with accessibility to power, water and handling the product that the structure shelters.

If bringing in water, electricity or a driveway is too costly for the budget at present, you will have to start weighing cost versus benefit. This can only be accurately done if you understand the requirements, choices and consequences.

- Drainage, ventilation and light requirements are also important considerations which change from location to location.

ORIENTATION

Orientation has to do with a structure being north/south, east/west, or somewhere in between.

This will have an impact on **ventilation**, **light**, **snow shedding** and **lay of the land**.

> For all of these things you need to have a good handle on what the structure needs to perform well.

A structure **must be level** from side to side to shed snow well but can have some slope from end to end.

IMPORTANT CONSIDERATIONS

Ventilation is easier when a structure is inline with the prevailing winds.

Building in line with the **prevailing winds** will be less stressful on your structure. Any snow loads which you will deal with are more likely to be balanced. When snow is significantly higher on one side than the other, it will have to be removed.

Keep in mind that **wind patterns and snow build up** will change once you put in a second or third building as well. A tree line is the only true wind break but it can cause problematic shadows. Putting the structure behind a barn or hill only makes things worse when you factor in the swirling. Exposure may be necessary for ventilation but it will make heating costs more expensive.

Dealing with **excess ground moisture** will be a HUGE problem going forward. There will always be issues of **excess humidity**. It is normal to have ground moisture as an issue the first year of any new structure. Adequate drainage is a vital consideration.

If your project includes **movable structure**, your planning must include all the topographical features for your property. Any excavation required is much cheaper before there is anything there. Some locations require **extensive excavation**. Some shapes work on slope, some need perfectly flat. In these scenarios, your base could get more complicated and costly.

SITE REQUIREMENTS

Safety is job #1. Make sure you have the required tools and that they are in good working order.

Make sure your shelter site is fairly level and well drained. Moderate lengthwise slope is acceptable. Replacement of the top soil with gravel in a non-growing application will increase drainage and minimize weeds. Building in line with the prevailing wind will create less wind action and stress on the building.

- Condensation and excessive moisture can be relieved with good drainage
- Putting down ground cover is an inexpensive way of eliminating grass and weeds while allowing drainage
    - This is not suggested for heavy foot traffic or where there is machinery movement

It is critical that this structure be mounted or installed level from side to side.

When significant excavation has been done, **the anchoring system MUST be set into concrete.**

The building pictured to the left is 120′ long and was going on an existing concrete bunker. 20′ of the building was "normal" and flat and the rest had a 4′ slope. The customer wanted a level structure. The issue was that as you cut something off the bottom of a hoop, the building gets narrower so the trick was to prevent that. This project gave me an opportunity to really understand the profile complexities of the buildings in great detail. By understanding these principles, I am better equipped to create solutions for other people's situations that are not always straight forward.

CHAPTER THREE: STRUCTURE SHAPES AND FRAMING

KEY TAKEAWAY: The shape and spacing of your framework are the key components in determining the capacity for wind deflection and snow shedding

Gothic structures have a rounded profile going up to a peak, with a ridge or spine. This shape has better snow shedding and more flexibility in width and height. It must be level from side to side.

Cathedral Shaped Structures take our standard gothic arch and flip it around to give more useable height, with less floor space (for RVs as an example). It is more susceptible to wind, because of the straighter sidewalls. No snow stays on this shape at all, unless there has first been a wet slushy rain/snow, and then a freeze

High Profile structures have straighter sidewalls than the Gothic profile, giving 2' more clearance than the standard Gothic shape. This allows you to get equipment closer to the edge or work easier in the building

Space savers are a combination of an A-Frame and a Gothic and are

particularly good for garages, as you are able to have more space for opening car doors and storage with less floor space. We usually discourage people from this shape since the steel has been significantly stressed with the tight radius bend and they do not perform as well in the winter.

<h1 style="text-align:center">SIZE CHOICES & CONSIDERATIONS</h1>

2. Pick a width: As you go wider, you need exponentially more steel and bracing which may or may not impact the ability to get engineered drawings. Generally speaking, when you go wider, the top will be lowered, unless you go to longer lengths of steel. The opposite is true for going narrower.

3. Pick a length: Any length is possible; simply by adding hoops If you are building between 2 fixed points, the last hoop spacing can be modified to fit the spot.

4. Pick a height: Building higher will improve the **snow shedding** characteristics of the building. Building higher gives more interior space close to the wall but the structure catches more wind. Since building higher catches more wind, the structure may require reduced hoop spacing. Building higher will be a little costlier to heat but does **improve natural air circulation**. Building lower will decrease snow shedding and may require closer hoop spacing.

Size is a three-dimensional choice. You can go

- wider or narrower

- longer or shorter

- higher or lower

- A fourth dimension could be heavier or lighter.

When you are picking a size of a structure, obviously, you must take into account your **immediate need**.

You must also consider **what will fit on the property**, particularly as to how that relates to some of your longer-range plans. Building a little longer now, is a lot cheaper than having to add to it in the future. Certain sizes simply lend themselves to expansion better than other sizes.

EFFICIENT USE OF AREA

30 x 30
= 900 sqft

20 x 45
=900
sqft

Roof & end surface approx. 2,200 sqft

Vs. Roof & end surface approx. 1,700 sqft

<u>Almost 25% difference</u>

When it comes to size, most of the time going longer and narrower is typically cheaper per square foot than going shorter and wider. It does not matter how simple your ends are, that cost for the ends is the same for 30' long or 300' long. Going longer is the cheapest way to expand.

When comparing the surface area of a 30x30 to a 20x45, both are 900sqft. When you include the roof and ends in calculating the surface area, on the 30x30, it becomes close to 2200sqft, as opposed to the 20x45 which has only about 1700sqft.

The one configuration has 25% more surface area! **These numbers will have a direct impact on heating costs.**

Going taller is more expensive to heat but sheds snow better. It also catches more wind.

Covers are 32' wide vs. 36'. **A difference of 12.5%**

COMPARING TALLER AND LOWER BUILDINGS

A taller building will **shed snow much more efficiently** than a lower unit. The load of piled up snow will be more vertical than lateral. 6' of snow against a high unit is not a problem. 4' of snow against a lower unit is risky.

The other trade-off is that the higher unit also **catches more wind**.

> Compare a puddle that freezes before a pond, a pond freezes quicker than a lake, a lake freezes quicker than the ocean. The smaller body of water reacts quicker than the bigger one. The same is true in reverse in the spring.
>
> In the summertime, a shallow pond always has algae on it, whereas a deeper body of water is clear.

Going taller is **more expensive to heat** because heat loss is in direct proportion to surface area exposed to outside.

> An **example**: a 20' wide building that is 10' high will have 32' of roof cover. A 20' wide building that is 12' high will have 36' of roof cover. Therefore, the high unit will be about 12.5% more expensive to heat. Since the high unit has bigger ends, that ratio gets worse.

On the positive side, the higher unit has a greater volume of air, and therefore the **temperature will fluctuate slower**.

This shows that the deeper body of water has **more natural circulation** than the shallow one. The same principle applies to air volume and movement.

Proper air circulation is critical for animals. It is easy to close up a building to maintain heat, but in reality, you are doing more harm than good. For animals, keeping them dry and out of the wind is 90% of the battle. Cold does not hurt them.

STRUCTURAL COMPONENTS

This is an overview of some of the main steel components of the structure, what makes up the skeleton or frame of the building

RIDGE

The ridge is the very top part (the spine) of your structure.
Stubs are welded on every 2, 3, 4 or 6 feet according to the requirements of your particular structure. It is onto these stubs that the hoops will be fastened.

RIDGE CROSS/STARTER

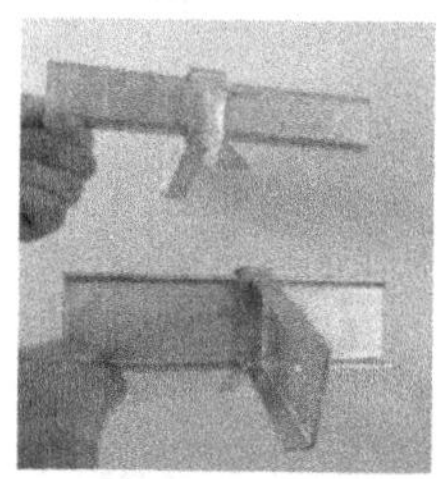

This photo shows the starter stubs for 1"x2" and 1"x3" hoops that is supplied by MSS, **usually preinstalled**, into the first ridge. This ridge is flipped around to connect in with the rest of the line of ridge pieces you will be installing. The ridge cross/starter is always used to join the first and second length of ridge together.

The diagram below depicts 4' spacing only. If you have 3' hoop spacing, you will have 4 pairs of stubs per ridge; 2' spacing has 6 pairs of stubs per ridge; and 6' spacing has 2 pairs of stubs per ridge.

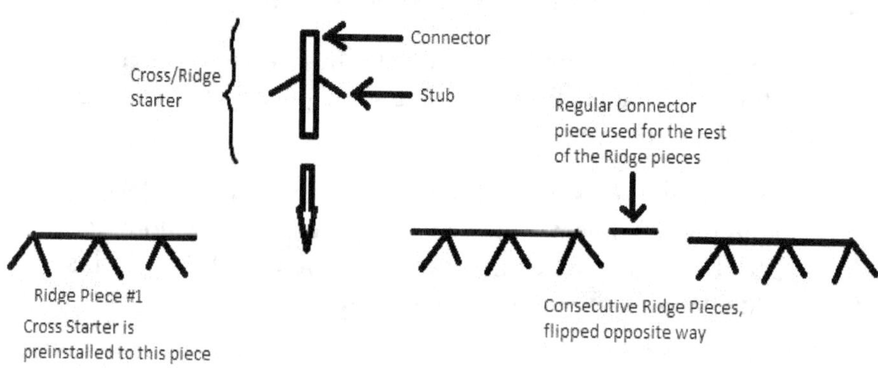

HOOPS

Note: Be aware of safety and use a scaffold for putting up the larger structures, especially when building the unit on a wall

General Notes: The curved part of the hoop is usually the bottom; the straight part goes to the peak. For structures that have been supplied as a cathedral unit (for RV, boats, etc.) the curved part goes up and the long straight part goes down.

Always put hoops up in pairs for better balance and stability.
Apply downward pressure on the top edge of the hoop.
The fastener ALWAYS goes horizontally.

If you are not sure, it is easy to "test" by laying a pair of hoops to the desired width. Stand the ridge against this. If it does not easily line up, you have it backwards.

Before continuing on the other <u>ridge</u> pieces, the purlins should be attached and then

<u>**IT IS CRITICAL** at this point to secure the structure in a vertical position with two guide ropes (inverted V).</u>

The guide ropes must go both ways as an inverted V and be secured with some sort of anchoring post to ensure everything stands vertical. If you do not plumb the building NOW, it will be much more difficult later.

PURLINS

Purlins are the horizontal spacers in between the hoops used to maintain rigidity in the structure. They are the lateral spacers between the hoops. Purlins are 1-1/4" diameter with both ends flattened and are fastened to the underside of the hoop with a purlin clip. The overall length is 1" more then the hoop spacing. Usually hoops up to 17' long have 1 row of purlins per side. Hoops that are 19' or longer have two rows of purlins per side.

> **IMPORTANT**
> wind braces are the longer pipes, purlins are the shorter ones

The holes drilled in each end are spaced at the same spacing as the hoop spacing.

The tabs with the holes of 2 purlins overlap and are bolted to the underside of the hoop (structure).

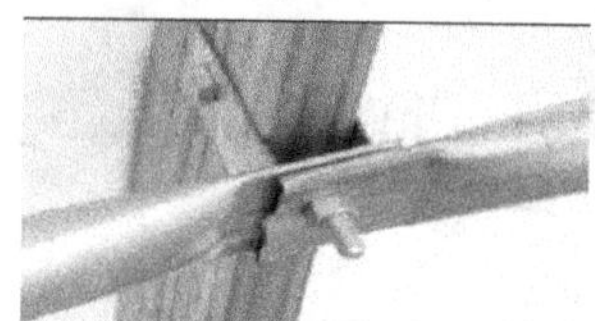

DO NOT install on the outside, they will prevent snow from sliding off and also create drip lines.

Be sure that the structure is standing perfectly vertical <u>before attaching the purlins.</u> Do not tighten completely at first until entire building is framed (use level to determine if building is leaning)

34

WIND BRACES

Wind Braces are the same material as purlins, except they are approximately 50% longer and go diagonally in each corner. By going from the purlins, diagonally down, the whole structure is braced. The quantity of braces per corner is determined by the size of the hoop, the spacing of the hoops and the quantity of purlins. 2 rows of purlins have double the quantity of braces that a single purlin structure has.

Wind braces look like purlins except they are about 50% longer. They are installed diagonally in all four corners AFTER the purlins have been secured.

A note about the length of the wind braces

The quantity of braces depends on the structure size and certain construction details. Usually the small structures have 1 per corner, mid-sizes have 2 per corner and larger structures have 3 or 4 per corner. **When building on a wall or in a very windy location, it may be advisable to double up on the braces.** Structures with 3' hoop spacing will have more, shorter braces.

Connect wind braces into the same purlin clip as the purlins. The bottom end of one wind brace is tied to the top end of the next wind brace using the purlin clip already there.

CROSS TIES

Cross-ties are the same material as purlins and wind braces but longer. They tie the left and right sides of the building together, usually on the same bolt as the upper row of purlins. The purpose of cross-ties is to stiffen a building under wind load and give more snow load strength.

They are usually 3' to 4' down from the peak. Many people look at cross-ties as a nuisance because of lost head space but they have a three-fold benefit.

- By forming the triangle at the peak, you create benefit for the dead load which is usually snow load. The top can not come down when the sides can not spread.

- By tying the left and right sides together, you create strength for the live load, commonly referred to as wind load. When the wind blows from the left, the right side holds it from pushing inward and vice versa.

- Most importantly, it decreases the rocking motion which can stress a building over time.

- The cross-tie can also supply a very useful support area for things that need to be suspended.

It is important to remember that when you spread out the load you create strength. Long cross-ties or cross-ties in heavy load areas will require mid support and lateral bracing. **Keep in mind that adding a cross-tie decreases the usable height of your building, usually by 24-36 inches**

Cross-ties are an inexpensive way to reinforce your structure, typically increasing the snow/wind load by 5 pounds per sq. ft.

They are made from the same material as the purlins and wind-braces and, depending on the width of the structure, between 10 and 14 feet long. In cases where the cross-ties are not included in the package they are available as add-ons.

They are installed under the ridge and span across the width of the structure from hoop to hoop.

Cross-ties are not normally supplied for the two end pairs of hoops since this would interfere with the end framing. They are strongly recommended to be purchased if your building is open ended.

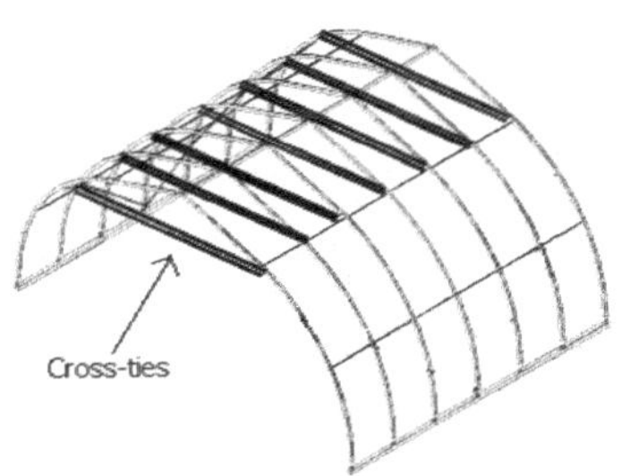

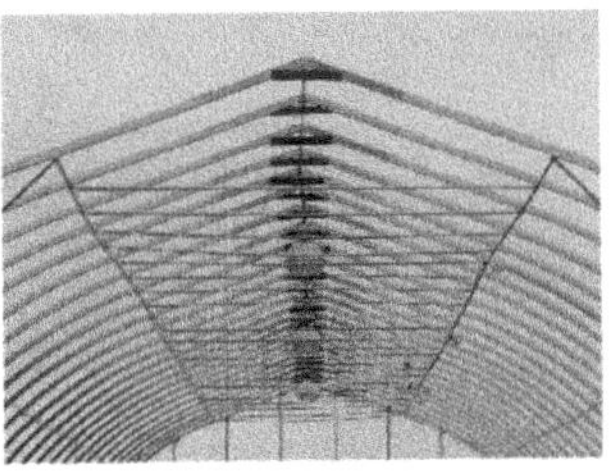

CHAPTER FOUR:
BASE AND FOUNDATION

> **KEY TAKEAWAY:** There is no such thing as too many anchors

ANCHORING CONSIDERATIONS: BASE AND FOUNDATION

1. **Pick a base or foundation: Base Brackets** fasten under each hoop to secure the building to a beam. This beam can be ground mounted or on blocks, posts, slab or shipping containers. Another option is a welded steel base rail if the structure needs to be moveable. The last option is **Anchor Posts**. Each hoop would sit on a post that may need to be set into concrete. These hollow steel tubes are 1 ¼" x 36" or 1 ¾" x 40". There is one anchor post per hoop, usually set into concrete. Anchor posts are not advisable for very heavy or stony ground because of shifting. Anchoring the foundation is critical to the long-term life of the building

**Please remember that there simply is
no such thing as too many anchors.**

Anchoring prevents a structure from settling under snow load, prevents lifting under aerodynamic forces and prevents shifting with wind forces. The vast majority of issues with structures have arisen from the structure not being anchored properly.

We offer two main types of anchoring for our structures: Base Brackets (left pic) and Anchor Posts (right pic). Which one you decide to go with largely depends on your application and location. They are not to be used together, it is a one or the other option. No matter which option you choose, please be aware, there is no such thing as too many anchors!

Proper anchoring will prevent your building from settling under snow load. It will prevent your building from becoming a parachute. It will prevent your structure from shifting to your neighbour's property.

Although the building can be anchored directly into the ground with Anchor Posts, it can also sit on a slab, curb or beam or it can be elevated on some sort of a wall. Base brackets with lag bolts are supplied standard to fasten the building to the chosen form of foundation. Anchor Posts are available at an additional cost.

Anchor Posts must be set into concrete when:

- the soil has been recently excavated (within the last 5 years)

- it is required by the building code (use of concrete usually classifies the building as permanent)

- extremely windy and exposed areas exist (at least use on the corner posts)

- more than 10% of the anchor post will be out of the ground (upgrading anchor post size may be needed)

- there are areas where erosion has been a problem in the past

Anchor Posts SHOULD NOT be used (and base brackets used instead) when:

- the soil is a very heavy clay (heaving would be a constant problem)

- there is a shallow rock layer

- there are major amounts of rocks interfering with the accuracy of anchor post setting

- the structure will be moved shortly (anchor posts must be cleaned out before reusing)

Consider the total surface area and friction the anchor can provide. Adding concrete will add friction and weight but also cost and permanence. Total surface area will also determine resistance to lateral shift. Many times, the direction of an anchor can either enhance or detract from the effectiveness of the anchor. Be aware of the total surface area in contact with the soil. This means that often, more smaller posts can have better holding power than fewer big posts.

Posts are more effective with cleats across the bottom, preferably going both ways. This way when the hole is filled with soil, there is much more than just friction on the post preventing it from being sucked out of the ground.

By putting a stringer on the inside and outside of the post, just below grade, you are no longer just relying on the surface of the post to prevent forces from either tilting or leaning in.

How does structure shedding rain affect the holding power of anchors?

We tend to think of the holding power of soil as to how it relates to compaction and drainage. The more it is packed, the better it holds. The better it is drained, the better it holds.

A 30' wide structure sheds rain and snow 15' each way. This means that the 1' strip along each side gets 15 times as much rain as the rest of the land!

If you do not have extremely well drained soil, it will have a fraction of the holding power. The area around the anchors turns to mush with little resistance to lateral shift or out tilt.

When you have recently disturbed soil, you will have to do extra work to give the posts the holding power they need. Most of the time, this "extra" refers to a lot of concrete.

When people want to insulate, it is suggested that they prepare the area beside the structure with a slight down slope and then put the insulation on top of that. Cover that with a thin layer of gravel. With this procedure, you will have less labour, less soil disturbance, it will keep the weeds away from the building and you will get all the benefits of frost protection.

BASE BRACKETS

Base Brackets are NOT used in combination with Anchor Posts

Although the building can be anchored directly into the ground, (see option: anchor posts) it can sit on a slab, curb or beam or it can be elevated on some sort of a wall. Base brackets with lag bolts are supplied to fasten the building to the chosen form of foundation.

Install the base brackets at spacing equal to the spacing of the stubs on the ridge (i.e.: 4' space between the stubs on the ridge, means 4' spacing of the base brackets. The lag bolts are installed in-line with the structure

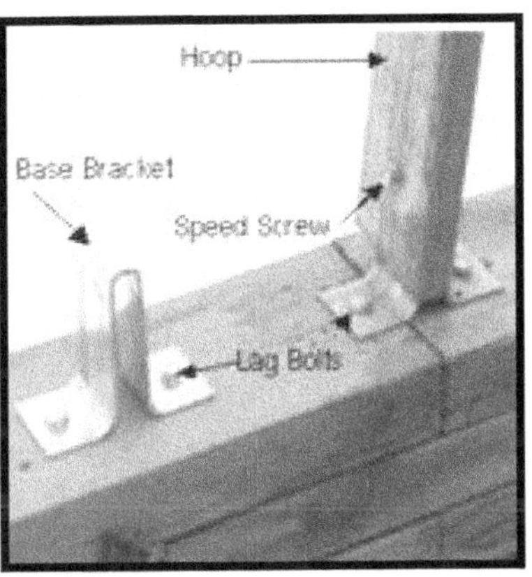

- The outside to outside measurement of the wall or beam should be slightly greater than the width of the building. (+3" for 1x2 hoops and +5" for 1x3 hoops)
- If the center of the base bracket is more than 2" from the edge, there will be a ledge where there is the potential for damage to the cover as the building is shedding snow or ice.
- The overall length of the beam or wall should also be an extra 4", unless you plan to have a solid end covering.

BASE BEAM

By using 3 layers of 2x6 rather than a 6x6 beam (as seen in the pic), you can create a continuous laminating effect by offsetting the layers. By trimming 1" off of the middle board, you get 2x6, 2x5, 2x6. This creates a "pocket" where the side of the cover can be secured.

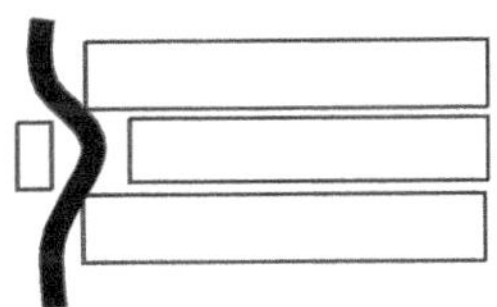

ANCHORING THE BEAM

- With the exception of the large concrete blocks, the base needs to be anchored to prevent lateral shifting and/or uplift.
- Spiral earth anchors or T-bars can be used to anchor beams (usually 2 per pair of hoops). Leaning these in an alternating pattern creates extra holding capacity.
- **Anchors MUST be to the inside of the beam**. In case of multiple beams (stacked) the anchor must be attached to at least two layers. **Rebar through the beams does not have sufficient holding power.**
- The AVERAGE spacing of your anchors should never be more than 4' unless you are in a forest. Towards the corners, the anchors are usually closer to each other and along the middle they can be slightly further apart.
- **There must be a minimum of 2 fasteners per post.**

SETTING WALL POSTS

Putting some concrete into the bottom of the hole significantly adds to the holding capacity. Posts should always be set below the frost line and have at least as much length below the surface as above.

- When auguring holes to set posts, extreme care should be exercised to pack the soil around the posts firmly.
- Spacing the posts further apart usually does not save any time or money since extra time will be spent packing the soil (also greater need for concrete) and a heavier sill plate will be required.
- There should be a horizontal board on the outside of the posts just below grade. This will give extra protection against posts leaning outward.

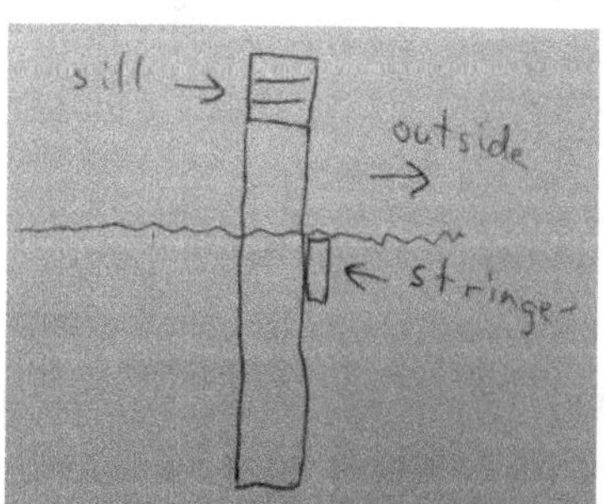

SILL PLATE

The sill plate bridges the gap between the posts or ties base beams together. In the case of a railroad tie it also gives consistency to the top surface to allow for level construction of the building. If the sill plate is capping something else (i.e. beam) then a 2x4 is sufficient. A 2x6 sill plate between posts is sufficient unless the post spacing is more than 4'. Unless you are building on a beam you should add a 2x4 on edge as a place to fasten the cover. The joints should always be offset to create extra strength. The outside to outside measurement of the sill plate is usually 4-5" more than the stated width of the building.

BASE BRACKET PLACEMENT

Place 2 parallel runs of the base brackets on the beam or wall. The center to center spacing between these lines is equal to the width of your building. The in line spacing is equal to the specified hoop spacing of the building you purchased. Each bracket is secured with 2 lag bolts which MUST be in line with the length of the building.

INSTALLING ANCHORS TO A BASE BEAM

The main function of anchors is to prevent uplift. Do not forget about the "foundation function" as well which is meant to prevent settling or lateral shifting. Improperly anchoring a building from up lift, down force and lateral movement will all, equally, cause problems and expense. There are many different ways of anchoring a building because there are so many circumstances which people are dealing with.

When anchors can be installed at opposing angles, they work against each other and therefore will multiply their holding power. Care must be taken to stay away from anchors that will bend (i.e. re-bar). When the anchors are going straight into the ground, care must be taken to ensure proper holding power. This is most often done with plugs of concrete. When anchors have been extended out of the ground, care must be exercised to eliminate the possibility of outward lean. It is important to consider the total number of square inches of contact area between anchors and soil. Many time fewer big anchors is less holding power.

Anchors are generally very inexpensive, especially when you are looking with hind sight at some damage.

STORAGE CONTAINERS AND CONCRETE BLOCKS
FOR A BASE

There has often been the need to elevate structures to create more storage capacity. When the product being stored does not lend itself to stacking, such as salt, sand or soil, there is the added dimension of outward push on the wall. Not only does the pile push outwardly, but an operator scooping the product will create even greater push.

Storage containers and **over sized concrete blocks** are the economical solution for such a storage requirement. The weight and the stability which both the containers and blocks give, eliminates the need to anchor into the ground. Containers are often simply put on the ground. When going more than two layers with the blocks, there should be a concrete pad or special preparation of the soil to provide stability.

When choosing this foundation method, it is important to consider how and where the shelter will shed water and snow. The top of the wall or container must be sealed to the possibility of moisture going inside. The other thing that must be given proper consideration is that the shelter is able to deal with the extra wind load created by elevating the shelter this much. In most of these installations, the wind load on a building is at least double of what it would be if mounted on the ground.

ANCHOR POSTS

Anchor Posts are NOT used in combination with Base Brackets
The base or anchoring system needs to be installed first. Please remember that our suggestions are based on years of experience, but ultimately it is your responsibility to meet local requirements and/or building code requirements. There is no such thing as too well anchored. Any extra time spent at this point is time well spent. Install the anchor posts at spacing equal to the spacing of the stubs on the ridge (ie: 4' space between the stubs on the ridge, means 4' spacing of the anchor posts.) The lag bolts are installed in-line with the structure

I had someone call me that half their building blew away. When I went to investigate, I happened to notice something set off to the side – a wheelbarrow full of off cut anchor posts. Since he couldn't get them all the way in the ground, he cut them off at the length it said to be exposed and this was why his structure blew away!

SETTING ANCHOR POSTS

1. Level the side to side area where your structure is to be erected. (A small end to end slope is acceptable).
2. Lay the ridge along your string line for a quick and accurate way of marking the post spacing. (the spacing of the posts will be the same as the spacing of the stubs on the ridge)
3. Use a chunk of hardwood to protect the anchor post tops from the blows of the sledge hammer. Anchor posts can also be pushed in with the bucket of a tractor. You must still provide hardwood protection for the top
4. Anchor posts will rotate as they are pounded down, this can be easily straightened with a pipe wrench (holes should face side to side). It is best to rotate them to the correct spot with about 2" to go and then finish the job.
5. The post top should be 3"-5" above grade.
6. If installing a 2x6 wood baseboard use pipe straps installed below bolt connection to hoop.
7. Having the holes of the anchor posts on a flat plane is CRITICAL to the straight construction of your building.

DAMAGED ANCHOR POSTS

If a post top becomes burred or bend a bit, simply hit them between two hammers to bring the width down to ¾" again. If the top of the post is not salvageable you can cut ½" to 1" off the top without further consequence.

If you encounter a large rock, you can cut a post back ONLY IF there are no more then 1 or 2 per side, if it is not one of the first 3 from the end AND you are not cutting more then 1/3 off the post. If an anchor post is deflected off the intended direction, it can be bent to direct in closer to its intended location.

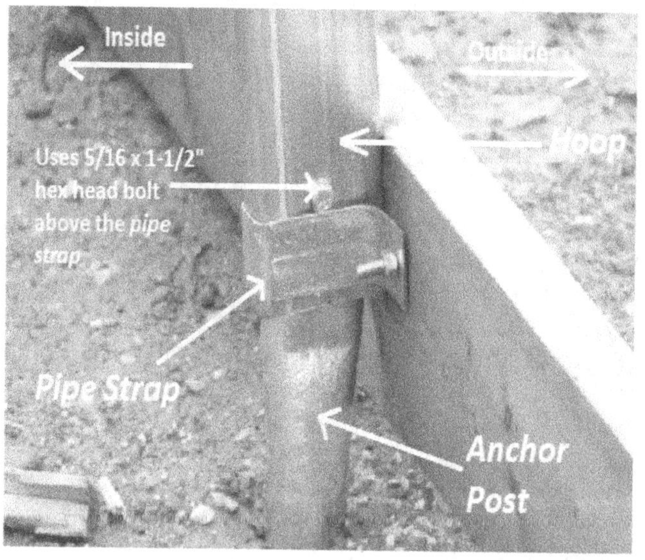

Anchor Post Details

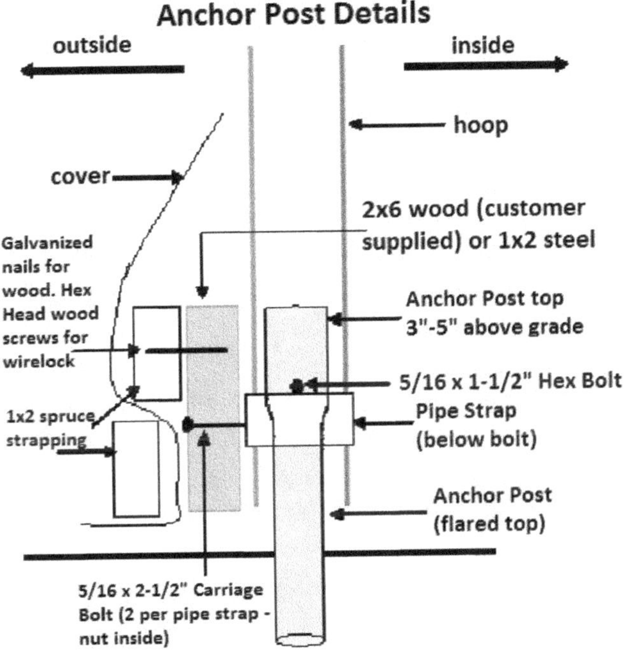

CHAPTER FIVE: COVERING CHOICES

KEY TAKEAWAY: As with any cover on any building, if the cover isn't properly secured and tight, there will be premature wear and tear

COVERING CHOICES AND CONSIDERATIONS

The easiest way to get a comparative cost of different covers is to take the replacement cover cost divided by the years of expected life span to get an annual cover cost.

6. **Pick a cover:** While considering your structure choices you will have to weigh cost versus benefit or return. There is no area which this is truer then with cover choices. The wide range of cover choices mainly include polyethylene and woven tarp products, and many more. Within each of these products there is an equally great variety of choices. Along with each of these choices there is a huge variation in cost and function or performance.

POLYETHYLENE PLASTIC

It is important to remember that plastic lasts longer than you should have it on.

The standard **covers** we offer are **6mil clear plastic which must be used for plants** and 6 mil white plastic which is used where shade is important but still need light (i.e.: livestock). Typical life span is 5-6 years.

Since the structures we offer are narrower and have a reduced hoop spacing, we can use a lighter cover of the options available.

Going clear (greenhouse) allows the necessary light transmission for plant growth. Clear plastic is also used for swimming pool covers, as both applications require sunshine to come through.

Going white (livestock) allows light while still providing a shade factor. It is slightly cooler inside the structure than the clear option. White plastic is also recommended for swimming pool applications where more privacy is required, as well as covering RVs or other equipment where fading would be an issue.

In 1974, plastic as a greenhouse cover was just being invented and getting multiple years out of it was something that was still being worked on. The owner where I was working decided that a structure we had could go for a second winter without changing the cover. During the second winter, something must have hit or touched the cover because it exploded. We spent several days picking up small fragments. Luckily covers last much longer and are easier to use now.

DOUBLE LAYER PLASTIC COVER

For greenhouses, swimming pools or livestock, we usually recommend a double cover, with roll up sides and an inflator fan. Double covers extend the life expectancy of the cover, reduce heat loss by 30%, which helps maintain the temperature in the structure, as well as reduce condensation. The small inflator fan that we offer and include in the double cover package prices, uses very little electricity and is left running all the time to keep air between the two layers so you can reap the benefits of the double cover. It is very effective for stiffening buildings in severely windy areas. The biggest attraction for the 6mil plastic is the life span you get for the investment.

TARP

Plants cannot grow under tarp.

Tarp is more expensive than the plastic options, but is also more durable if animals, equipment, car doors or hay might bump against the cover frequently. Our 12mil white woven covers have a much greater tear resistance then plastic. By providing shade, the white tarp is cooler in the summer. By still letting light in, it is warmer in the winter. We offer a green tarp as well but due to the heat it absorbs, the life span is typically 3 years less than white. It generally runs between 45¢-50¢/sqft depending on the size piece you require. Life expectancy is 5-6 years for the **green tarp** and 8-10 years for the **white tarp.** Green tarp comes with a 4-year warranty and white tarp a 6-year warranty against deterioration by the sun.

The green tarp consists of a green, black and white layer, which absorbs heat significantly more than our white option, which consists of a white, clear and white layer. The heat absorption contributes to faster deterioration of the green cover as well as having a higher inside temperature. The white tarp is less noticeable in the summer than the green is in the winter, if camouflaging is a concern. The white tarp also lets light in, making it easier to work inside the structure because it's not as dark inside. Tarps are fully waterproof.

Everyone wants to save money but they also want value for the dollars invested. Both of these plastic and tarp choices are by no means the heaviest that are out there, but they do provide excellent life span for the investment.

When you consider the cost per year on the 12mil white tarps, they stack up very favourably to the 20-24mil covers that are available. The main reason 12mil is even an option for us to use is that our hoops are much closer together and therefore provide much more support to the cover.

> **Having some extra people to quickly get the cover over and tacked down, insures that the job will be a success. At that point, the extra people can go if they need to.**

Regardless of which covering will be installed on your building, the success or failure of the job, and your safety, will often be determined by the **preparation and understanding of the task ahead.**

√ The effect of wind, even a breeze, will be magnified by the size of your cover. You will be looking at this cover for a long time, wait an extra day if necessary. Early morning or late evening is usually best time of day. The evening before or after a full moon are also often very calm

√ If your ends are covered in plastic it is definitely easier to do the ends before the roof cover goes on. This is because the end plastic normally goes UNDER the roof plastic. At the very least it is recommended to have the end wall framing in place before the roof cover goes on.

The lifespan of a cover can very quickly be reduced if it is repeatedly flapping in the hard wind.

<u>**Taking a short cut will leave you with more wrinkles**</u>.
Areas with wrinkles will flutter more and cause stress points.
This will also cause the cover to deteriorate quicker.

If you have never installed these covers before, it is recommended to use at least 4 people. After the bottom of the end cover has been

secured, pull the end cover over the hoop first. Person "A" will hold
it from the **inside** of the structure in such a way that there are no
wrinkles. The roof cover can now go over the channel as well.
 Person "B" will pull on the roof cover while person "C" installs the
stainless spring steel wire inserts. "C" will start from the peak and
work down. It is critical to remember that "A" and "B", who are
pulling on the two respective covers, must always be pulling at least
a foot ahead of "C" who is installing the wire insert. This will allow
a little give in the covers so that there will not be damage. With more
experience "B" and "C" can be done by one person.

 It is **CRITICAL** when fastening a cover, that the cover is
fastened tight LENGTHWISE at the peak BEFORE
tightening the sides

When you are tightening the cover, you should **always pull 90
degrees to the wrinkle.** This means that after you have secured at
the peak, most often you will be pulling diagonally to the corner.

When you are covering the ends of the structure, there are some
similarities and some fundamental differences when you are covering
with plastic or with tarp. The aluminium wirelock channel must be
installed on the top side of the hoop before you start the cover. You
start at the base of one side and go continuously over the peak so that
there is not an edge at the peak. Your cover will be a rectangle and you
must double check if the two ends were supplied as one piece or not.
The framing must also be in place before you are putting on the cover.

The cover gets fastened, temporarily, at the base first on either side of
the door and then pull out to the corners. If there is ANY wind, do into
the wind side first. Please remember that
whenever you have wrinkles or folds, you
will pull 90 degrees to the wrinkle. Excess on
the end covers will only get trimmed off after
the roof cover is on as well.

56

If you are covering the end with plastic, you would go with the extra of your rectangle and fasten it temporarily to the back side of your framing. At the very most, at this stage you will put part of a wire insert on either side of the peak. When the cover is sitting smooth, you can put some strapping on the vertical framing to hole the cover in place.

If you are covering the ends with tarp, you will need to remove the wirelock channel first. This may seem like double work, but the channel is now curved to the building with the required screw holes. The end tarp cover is sandwiched between the hoop and the bottom of the wirelock channel. When you pull the tarp over the peak, you will reinstall the wirelock channel from the top and work down. If you do the left, right or bottom first will be determined by where the wrinkles are (if any).

I got a call in the middle of winter one year, from a customer complaining about damage to their 27x144 greenhouse. Upon review, I saw there was significant buckling that was challenging to understand. When I asked the customer how hot it was when they installed the cover, their response was 104°F. Then I asked how many people helped put the cover on, their response was about 10. So, I realized they got the cover on drum tight on the hottest day of the year. The cover had contracted nearly a foot! There wasn't anything that could be done until spring.

WIRELOCK (WIGGLE WIRE)

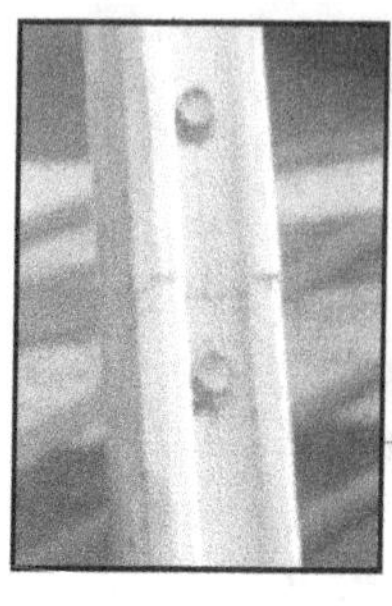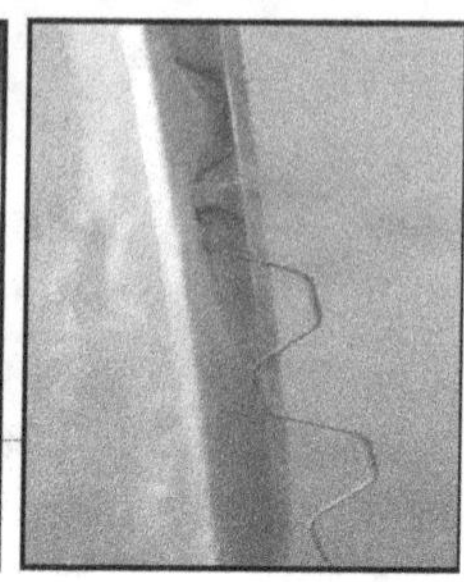

The beauty of wirelock is its ability to hold multiple layers of covers, even covers in different directions (i.e. roof and ends or 2 long lengths). Before starting you must at least have the cover tacked at the opposite end. This will give you resistance for pulling the cover tight. Our wirelock channel will hold up to 3 layers of 6 mil plastic securely. Two layers of 12 mil tarp will not be held securely in the wirelock channel. This is why we recommend that the top of the end wall tarp be sandwiched between the channel and the hoop.

It is also important to remember the wrist technique for installing the wire insert. Do not slide the wire straight back and forth. This causes abrasions on the cover. As you move back and forth, apply pressure with the thumb on the next parallel spot of the wire insert. Use a needle nose pliers to get the last tip into the channel. The next wire insert does not have to be overlapped.

Most buildings come with enough wirelock to be installed on top of the first and last hoop. Additional wirelock can be purchased to run along the sidewall, or to be used to attach the covering to the end framing or doors if desired.

The end wall tarp is sandwiched between channel and hoop, inserts hold the roof tarp in place. By installing the end channel and then removing it to install the end cover, your channel will be pre-bent and have the correct holes.

SIDE WALL COVER FASTENERS (you have 3 choices)

Notes: Pipe Straps are supplied when a structure has roll-up side walls and/or anchor posts options. When base board (wood or steel) is fastened with pipe straps, the base board should be pushed in so that it butts into the last hoop

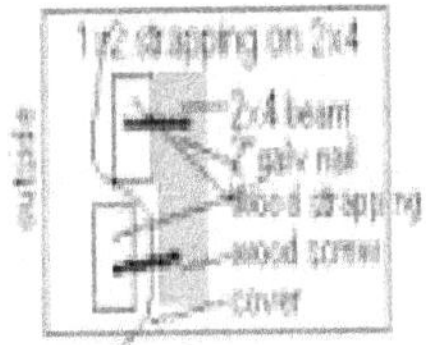

Only *pipe straps* & fasteners are supplied. Nails and screws for strapping are not supplied. 1x4 Wood for the top of the *roll-up side* is adequate.

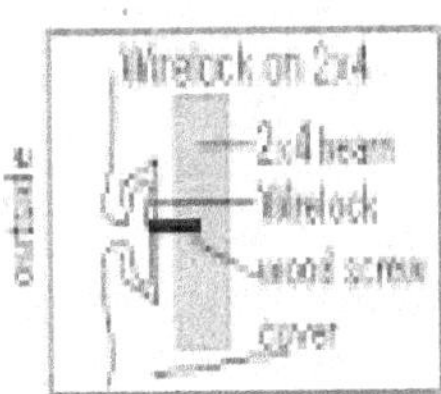

Pipe straps & fasteners and wood screws (12" centers) for the *wirelock* channel are supplied

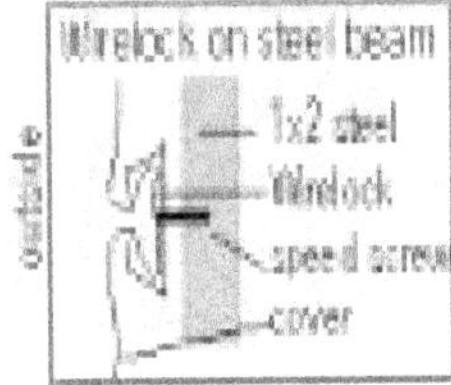

All required materials & fasteners are supplied. Steel #14 screws & *wirelock* (#12 screws not recommended as the base when used with the *roll-up* option)

INFLATOR FAN

An inflator fan is a **very** small fan which is attached to the inner layer of a double layer structure cover. Because the inflator is a squirrel cage type of fan, it can run continuously against the back pressure it has created without overheating.

The primary benefit of the process of putting air between the two layers of cover is to reduce heat loss. By having this cushion of "insulation", the building experiences a significant reduction in condensation. The air-filled pockets act as a shock absorber therefore substantially stiffens the building in very windy locations. Covers tend to last longer since they are always tight.

The closer you are to achieving dead air space, the more these benefits can be maximized. 4"-5" of air space is optimum. Too much air space will result in air movement and reduced efficiency. When installing a double cover, both layers are on the outside of the structure but only the inside layer is pulled tight.

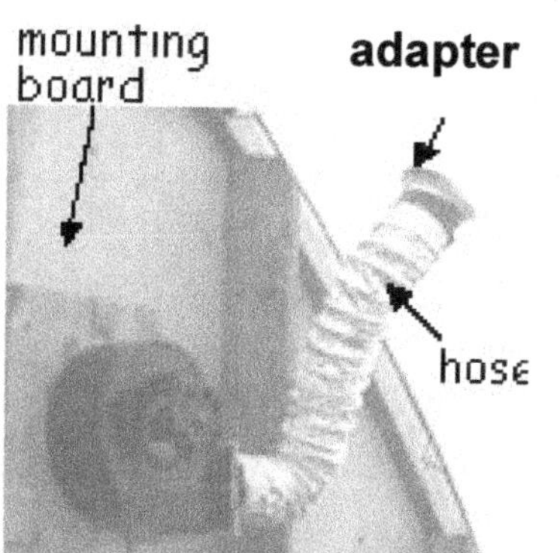

An inflator fan is a small blower which puts air in between two layers of roof cover on a greenhouse or livestock shelter. Benefits of inflator fans are:

- to achieve some degree of heat efficiency (up to 30% reduction in heat loss).
- virtually eliminates condensation (by insuring that there are no holes in the cover and making sure the edges are sealed, you will create the dead air space required)
- ensures the cover is always tight since you simply get more air during warm weather
- creates longer cover life since nothing is ever rubbing on anything.
- reduces wind stress on the structure since it acts as a shock absorber.

The best location for the inflator fan is the corner from which the prevailing wind comes, usually the north or west side. (suggestion only)

Usually the unit draws inside air. If you are in a very high humidity application, it would be advisable to draw outside air.

Most inflator fans come with a hanger plate rather than a mounting board. The mounting bracket of the fan can be fastened to the end framing or to the end hoop. The direction of the output is determined by convenience.

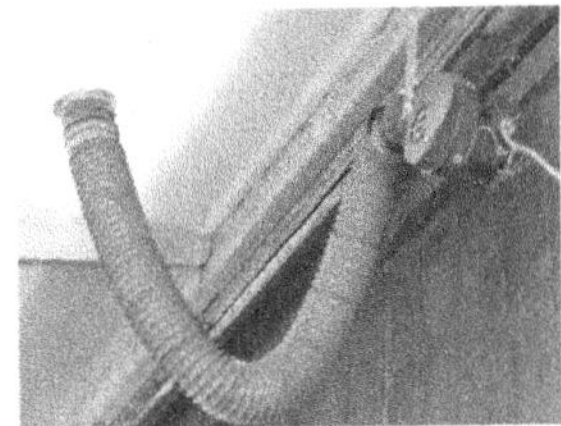

The motor shaft **MUST be horizontal** because of the type of bearings used.
Plug the fan in for a few seconds to make sure it is working properly. The adapter is usually attached 2' to 3' down from the ridge and 1' to 2' in from the outside edge. A double output fan has the adapters secured equal distance from the ridge.

SOLAR POWERED INFLATOR FAN

We have been continuing to get many inquiries about **solar powering the inflator fan** for greenhouses and livestock buildings. For the last year, we have been experimenting with a solar collecting package to determine what is required.

The first thing that must be emphasized, is that **you MUST use a squirrel cage type of fan and not a propeller type**. The propeller type cannot continuously run against back pressure.

The output required will be determined by the size of the greenhouse or livestock building. Our regular 110-volt fan draws .25 amp and puts out 80 cfm. Some small buildings can use a smaller fan and some of the bigger ones require our double output fan which gives 130 cfm.

Our inflator fan works quite well going through an invertor. Any 12 or 24 volt fans which we have tried have been extremely noisy and therefore not feasible.

The biggest challenge which we encountered, is that the specific time the fan is needed the most for heat insulation, is also the time where there is the least capacity for generating power.

We used a single solar collector and a single battery and there was simply not a quick enough capacity for the battery to hold charge when we had several consecutive cloudy days in December/January

To add another solar collector to an already fairly expensive package, really becomes prohibitive and can deter from moving forward with it.

SOLAR INFLATOR FAN ALTERNATIVE

Based on this experience, we wanted to offer an alternative that balanced economy with feasibility. We have come up with a way where the extra roof plastic can be used on the inside of the structure.

This means that you **would not need the inflator fan but still have the effect of double plastic** with the air pocket for better heat efficiency. This system does require a bit of extra "fiddling" but the net cost will be a little less.

1. The structure is covered with a single layer of plastic just the same as you would if you were only doing a single layer.
2. Take the second piece of plastic inside the structure and fold it double lengthwise.
3. This double plastic will be attached to the underside of the ridge using the same aluminium as you would use to fasten the plastic to the roll up pipe.
4. Next remove the purlins from the one side of the structure and after you have pushed over the plastic, reinstall the purlins under the plastic. You will be pushing the bolts through the plastic.
5. The plastic will be fastened with wirelock to the underside of the end hoops.

We have already had some customers try this out and are very happy with the result. Please call us with any questions or to discuss your specific application and situation where you might use this. We would be happy to help you with your project!

CHAPTER SIX: VENTILATION CHOICES

KEY TAKEAWAY: It is critical to realize that all plants and animals have a threshold temperature where things stop functioning and to ensure this is factored in when creating a proper ventilation system

VENTILATION CONSIDERATIONS

Ventilation can either be done **passively through openings or mechanically with fans.**

7. Determine ventilation: Roll up Side Walls are an economical add on to our greenhouses or livestock shelters to provide natural ventilation.

- No electricity needed with simple hand crank & stop

- Variable height possibilities according to wind area

- Roll up sides work best in combination with end vents located near the peak

- Unique locking strip that is guaranteed not to slip or become out of alignment

Roof vents and exhaust fans are available options

Properly venting a building is a critical consideration when planning your building. Getting rid of the initial ground moisture, quickly, when you have erected your new shelter is something many people do not think of. Quality air changes for plants or animals is something that automatically comes to mind. Getting rid of moisture is equally as important for storing your valuables.

Since warm air holds moisture and warm air rises, it is important to have **venting capacity as high as is possible.**

Venting **through** the roof, with individual turbines or a continuous roof vent, is the most effective but also the costliest. This is only really necessary when you are in a very protected spot and there is a real need to keep the temperature down in a long building.

VENTILATION AS SEASON EXTENSION

To make your structure more of a year-round functioning entity, there are two main areas in which you have to make the structure more efficient-Heating and Ventilation.

1. **Heating** is normally not a large expense unless you are doing a greenhouse through the winter. Double plastic with air in between will have a stabilizing affect against wind and elements even when you are not heating. It will also give you 5° more margin for cold.

The more **dead air space** between these layers you can create, the closer you will be to achieving a 30% **reduction in heat loss**. Holes will result in air movement and therefore less efficiency. 3"-5" consistent space is ideal. It is a given that you would have less then that around the edges and over the ridge.

Double plastic will have a considerably longer **life span** and create greater temperature consistency in the building.

As stated previously, you must resist the urge to seal up the building to save heat. Proper air changes are much more important no matter what you are protecting

2. **Ventilation** is also one of your biggest considerations for the warmer times of the year. Ventilation can be done through **forced** or mechanical methods or **passive** through vents or roll up sides.

Vents are extremely effective since they can be placed higher up where the heat needs to be expelled. **Mechanical ventilation** is costlier both up front and to operate but it is easier to control since it is attached to a thermostat. For mechanical ventilation to be effective, it needs to be sized and located properly.

Climate control is especially challenging in the spring and the fall since most days you will have the need for both ventilating and heating.

One area that you need to be especially aware of is **stagnant air**. Without proper air movement, circulation and exchanging, stagnant air can cause many different types of diseases. It is important to understand what your requirements are.

CENTER PIVOTING GABLE VENT OPTION

We are pleased to introduce our center pivoting gable vent as a simple solution to the challenges of venting a building. For venting to be effective, it has to be as high as possible. This is a cost-effective alternative to costly roof vents.

Part of the window swings in and part of it goes out. Because of this, rain is never an issue and the window is easy to control even in extreme winds. Incoming air is always deflected up to mix with the warmest air. The tubular steel construction makes it both lightweight and resist twisting over time.

A continuous rope goes from the top of the window to a pulley at the ridge, down to ground level and back up to another pulley and then to the bottom of the window. By tying the rope off to an eye bolt on a gable post, this allows for very simple control from ground level.

Most medium length buildings that have the ends facing into the prevailing winds, can be adequately vented with gable end peak vents. Make sure that these openings are as big as possible and as high as possible. It is also important to make sure your "windows" can withstand the winds in your area. Our centre pivoting gable vent has filled this requirement very effectively. With part of the window going in and part of it going out, the wind can never get hold of it. With the top and bottom rope through a double pully on the ridge, it is easy to maintain precise control over the opening area

ROLL UP SIDES

Roll up sides are less costly and simpler to install but are restricted by the fact that you have to be there to open and to close.

Roll up sides are an economical way of getting lots of air movement since no electricity is required. Roll up sides become even more effective when used on longer buildings. Roll up sidewalls are often used in combination with a small exhaust fan for early and late season ventilation when opening the sides is not practical.

I went to a customer one time and his greenhouse was installed but the roll up sides were not working yet. I was checking the greenhouse out to see if everything was done properly. I noticed a hummingbird laying dead on the floor, so I picked it up. While I was holding it, I realized it wasn't dead, just overcome by heat. I went outside with it, put it on my finger and as it started reviving I could feel a bit of pressure from its claws on my finger. When it revived enough to start flying, it hovered for about 15-20 seconds about 20" away from my face as if to say thank you and it flew away. This is why it is imperative to have ventilation in a greenhouse because it can get hot!

If a structure is very exposed, it is best not to open the roll up sides more than 3' in height due to potential of wind damage. If a structure is extremely sheltered, it is best to go even up to 6' to create maximum opening. Roll up sidewalls are most effective when used in combination with peak end wall vents to create a "chimney effect" to draw warm air out of the building, especially when it is very calm. These vents are effective for air movement when outside temperature does not allow opening of the sides.

When a structure has a low profile, you will need to be careful during rainy periods due to moisture getting into the structure area. High profile structures (with straighter walls) usually work better with roll up sidewalls. When preventing a floor draft is an issue, the roll up mechanism can be raised and then the structure is lined with a skirt for the bottom 2'-3'. When using this method of ventilation, it should always be done on both sides. An effective use of this method includes opening the "downwind side totally and the opposite side on marginally.

People will often use netting to cover the rolled up area, if they have animals they do not want to escape.

Installing the top of the roll up wall at 4' above the grade is considered average.
2' – 3' is suggested for very windy and exposed areas, 5' – 6' works better for very sheltered locations.

If you have a **DOUBLE COVER**, in at least one place per side, you should cut off 6"-12" of the strapping and install that piece separately. This will allow you to remove this section to let the air from the top escape to the sides at the appropriate time. Or you can run a "jumper hose" from the inflated top to the rollup area in order to inflate the lower area when needed.

CHAPTER SEVEN: ENDS AND EXTRAS

KEY TAKEAWAY: Extreme care must be taken if one end is open and one end is closed. It is not recommended.

By building the ends according to your needs your new building can and will truly prove useful.

It is important to remember that you need to be very careful when you have one end closed and the other end open. When one end is closed, you could potentially create a "parachute effect" (trapping air, creating lift) and put a lot of added stress on your building and especially the cover.

> One of our customers was using a 20x32 building on a short wall to house sheep. He had one end open and one end closed, contrary to my cautions. The building was hit with a microburst and when the customer came to check, there wasn't a trace of the building. The unharmed sheep were now in a paddock without a roof.

When planning ends, it is important to have sufficient vertical framing to support wind load, doors, fans, etc. The spacing between the vertical framing will be determined by the amount of opening space required for the doors, etc. It is important to remember that where ever possible, framing needs to go from top to bottom. In the event of large openings, the related framing will need to be doubled or tripled.

It is also important to remember that when you are covering your end with tarp, the top end of the cover is sandwiched between the wirelock channel and the hoop. When you are covering with plastic, you will be fastening the top end inside the channel with the roof cover even if your roof is a double layer.

CONSIDERATIONS FOR END OPTIONS

There are as many ways of framing an end wall as there are customers, making it virtually impossible to come up with a detailed set of assembly instructions for each case. Other than a few basic principles to keep in mind, what does the job for you is the best way.

1. **CLOSED OR OPEN END** – The combination of some uses and structure shapes make open end(s) desirable since the entire end would be a door-way and a rectangular frame door is not big enough.

74

<u>A WORD OF CAUTION</u>

Extreme caution must be exercised if the intention is one end permanently closed and the other open. If the open end is facing the prevailing wind, you are setting yourself up for problems if there is no capacity for incoming air to escape.

2. **WOOD OR STEEL FRAMING** – for most people, wood is easier to work with and less costly. The down side is that it doesn't last as long as steel. Generally, **the larger the building the larger the framing**. The larger the framing, the further it can be spaced. **Framing must also be sized to the weight it will carry** (i.e. fans, doors).

3. **COVERING TYPE** – in our packages the end covering is usually the same as the roof, either clear plastic, white plastic or woven tarp. These are very inexpensive but not as durable, especially when there is a lot of handling. We can also supply Lexan or Dyneglass where appearance, long life and light transmission are important. This is a hard honeycomb/corrugated plastic material many use for ends. Plywood or sheet metal can be installed where appearance, long life and non-light transmission are important.

4. **CLOSED ENDS OR DOORS** – requirements are usually determined by accessibility requirements. Inside hinged or sliding doors are not restricted by snow on the ground but do require inside space to move. Sliding doors on the outside can extend past the building but are harder to seal. Roll-up tarp doors are low cost for the size opening they provide but are usually a little higher maintenance and cannot be sealed easily

5. **OPENING REQUIREMENTS FOR FORCED OR NATURAL VENTILATION** (if required) need to be considered BEFORE starting to close an end. Fans and louvres will also limit your choices of doors.

END WALLS: COVERING AND FRAMING

DOOR OPTIONS AND IDEAS

Hinged and sliding doors should be made from welded tubular framework to keep them light and resistant to twisting. The door cover is usually the same as the rest of the end although with a plastic covered end consider going with something solid (plywood, sheet metal, fiberglass, etc.) Welded door frames are usually, but do not have to be, rectangular in shape

1. **HINGED DOORS** should **ALWAYS have the hinges off-set in such a way that the door can swing all the way open**. The door post to which the hinge is secured should be at least a 4x4. A doorstop strip should be part of the header so that the door cannot swing through. The opening for hinged doors should be ½" bigger than the door. Hinged doors are susceptible to problems related to frost related shifting

2. **SLIDING DOORS** should be 1"-2" bigger than the opening to allow for sealing. The track should be fastened to the side of the header and be 50% longer than the width of the door. If the track extends more than 2' past the curve of the building, the end should be supported. It is usually desirable to slide a double door in one direction rather than splitting it because sealing the middle against drafts is very difficult.

3. **ROLL-UP DOORS (hard cover)** should usually be installed by the door manufacturer. They will tell you what opening and framing is required. The weight of the door is usually not a problem for the structure.

4. **ROLL-UP DOORS (soft cover)** should have two cross members attached to the tarp to prevent it from blowing inward. One is attached at the bottom and one in the middle. The middle one is attached to the cranking mechanism. There are also two verticals standing in front of your door posts with a space of 3" to prevent the door from billowing outward. **The of sealing the edges is the main issue with this system.**

5. **ACCORDION DOORS** are available up o 16' wide. There is much more substance to these doors than option #5, since there is a cross member every 2' sliding in a fixed track. The winch to crack this up is usually inside the structure but can be done outside as well.

6. **END WALL REMOVAL** is an option if the intention is to seal up the building for the winter and then to have total access the remainder of the year. Installing an extra wire insert in the wirelock channel will allow simple removal of the end, while numbering the framing pieces will simplify the re-assembly.

7. **SCISSOR DOOR** The framing of a scissor door consists of 2 vertical pieces of round steel which pivot on the hoop, immediately to the left and right of the ridge. The plastic is fastened to the "door posts" with the MSS roll up strip and along the hoop with the wirelock. The vertical framing will swing out until it matches the top profile of the hoop. This is not a solution for areas prone to significant winds. The advantage of the scissor door is its simplicity and ability to open most of the end.
A word of caution about the scissor door. It is only an option in a very sheltered location.

Hinged Doors

Sliding Doors

Soft Cover Roll-up Door

Accordion Door

PART TWO:

IMPORTANT CONSIDERATIONS

CHAPTER ONE:

WINTER AND YOUR STRUCTURE

> **KEY TAKEAWAY: Never go in a building where there has been obvious stress. When the snow load is balanced, the buildings can carry quite a bit of snow. However, it only takes a small amount of unequal snow load to cause significant problems. Early removal is key.**

SNOW LOAD AND CONSIDERATIONS

When the snow load is balanced, the buildings can carry quite a bit of snow. However, it only takes a small amount of unequal snow load to cause significant problems. When prevailing winds always hit one side of the building, there will always be more snow on the back side.

Unequal snow loading can lead to structure compromise or even failure.

Another way you can get an unequal snow load is by building the structure on a slope from side to side. The purpose of the gothic shape of the building is to encourage the snow to slide off. If one side is higher than that other, it creates the effect of one side being flatter than the other. If the flatter side is also the sunnier side, you simply aggravate the situation.

When assessing the amount of snow a building will hold, one area that is often overlooked is how it got there. If you are attaching a structure directly to a higher building there can be some funny drifting that could be a problem.

Another thing is that 100 pounds of snow may not be much for a building to handle, but if it suddenly lets go from a higher building, the same snow could hit with a force of 300 pounds.

> I had a customer who was paranoid about the snow load and put up a 30x120 on 2' spacing on a wall. The one year the drifting was so bad, he could snowmobile over the top of the structure and it was still okay!

The longer that the straight part of the hoop is going to the peak, the slower the structure will shed snow. The snow that builds up on the side from the structure shedding snow will also create lateral pressure. The more of the wall that can be vertical, the more the building will withstand that pressure.

REMOVING SNOW

When there is a lot of snow on the building, it is important to remove snow from the top or center before going along the outside with a snow blower. If you live in a heavy snow area, it is important to have the structures far enough apart that proper snow removal can be undertaken.

Especially when bumping off ice, it is important to start from the top and work down. Starting from the bottom will give the top extra opportunity for coming down. It is important to remove snow in a balanced pattern. Do some from one side, and then from the other side. Removing all the snow from one side can cause the building to shift and fail.

> Years ago, in January, 1990, when I was still doing installations, I was up in Armstrong, ON. I had one of my most memorable experiences getting to see the Northern Lights in full colour, everywhere. It was breathtaking. Our structures still stand proudly up to Northern Ontario winters. That trip I also had the offer by a local to be taught how to survive outside so I could save the cost of a motel room. I kindly declined.

There always seems to be so much pressure and panic to get a building before winter. The only thing that is important to get done sooner than later is the foundation work. **There will be lots of decent weather days between fall and Christmas to get the job done.**

If you think that it is too late to get it done and you will simply wait until next spring, please remember that you said the same thing last spring (or even a few months ago) and as usual the busyness of life got in the way.

For those of you who want to get the structure up now and cover it in the spring, we urge you to cover the building sooner than later for a couple of reasons.

1. First is that there will be lots of other things vying for your time in the spring

2. Secondly, the more snow you have on that spot which has to melt, the more moisture you will have in the building. The more moisture you have in the building the more <u>condensation issues</u> you will have. You want to give that ground the most time possible to dry up before you need to start using the building.

Even though putting the cover on in late fall or early winter is more difficult and not pleasant, the benefits of having more time for the ground to dry, far outweigh the time spent to adjust the cover in the spring

When dealing with freezing rain, it is important to note that the ice in itself is not an issue, even a very thick layer actually has enough strength to become self-supporting.

There are two potential problems though.

- If the ice stays on the building, it usually has a rough enough texture that subsequent snow will not likely slide off. This scenario lead to major problems previously when we had freezing rain, followed by a dump of snow and then we had rain. This can triple the weight on a building in very short order.

- The other potential problem happens when you are attempting to remove the ice from the building. If the ice layer is not too significant you can gently bump the cover from the inside.

ALWAYS start bumping the cover from the top.

This way ice will slide over ice. Starting from the bottom creates a potential where the ice sliding down will fall back against the building and slash the cover.

NEVER do all of one side and then the other.

Work both sides simultaneously. If there is the slightest doubt in your mind about the amount of weight on the building, bump the cover from the outside using something with a long handle.

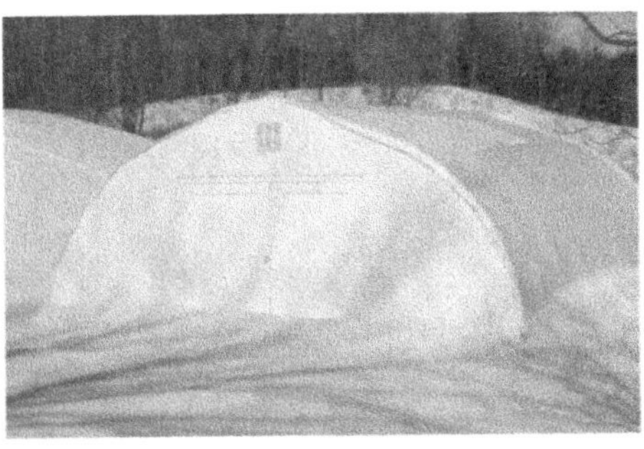

The buildings we manufacture are not industrial grade shelters and, as such, some caution must be exercised under some winter storm conditions….

Although the shelters are peaked to encourage the snow to slide off, some freezing rain and wet snow conditions will cause a build-up. Extra hoops or thicker steel are an economical way to increase wind and snow load capacity. Heavy duty models can include hoops at 3' spacing, or even 2' spacing if this is a concern for you.

The gothic shape with a slippery cover is designed to be lightweight and snow **resistant**. This encourages the snow to slide off quickly.

Snow removal, when occasionally required, is a simple task. Uneven snow loading is deceiving, since the total weight is not a problem but the lateral force can cause the hoops to distort. It is rare to have any significant snow build up on the roofs; however,

Everyone knows they aren't supposed to put their tongue on a cold sign post. A variation of that happened to me while I was installing a greenhouse years ago up in Armstrong. As I was lining up a bolt with the hole, I put the nut in my mouth. It took about a minute for it to let go

DO NOT GO INSIDE A BUILDING WHERE THERE HAS BEEN OBVIOUS STRESS!

Be aware of these scenarios where excessive snow build up is possible and damage could follow:
A wet snowfall followed by dropping temperatures
A building 90° to the prevailing wind (drifts could form on the backside of the building)
A building attached to and situated downwind of a taller building (significant drifting)

A building 90° to another building that has a higher roof, could cause a surge in snow weight when the snow on the upper roof slides off.

Preventative measures for excessive snow build up (where possible):

Build structures in line with the prevailing wind
Build structures level from side to side to create uniform shedding
Do not attach your building to a larger existing building
Install a heat source to melt the snow

Economical additions to increase your structure's snow resistance:

Install cable or tubular cross-ties at each pair of hoops, to create a triangle (when using cables there is no need to put them under tension)
Place wooden or metal support posts under the ridge. These can be suspended from the ridge with no more than ½" ground clearance. This will provide support as soon as there is load and structure movement will not dislodge your supports.
Use closer hoop spacing for the first 12' section away from another bigger building

Pointers for removing snow:

NEVER remove all the snow from one side and then the other
Remove the snow off the top of your building before using a machine (snow blower, etc.) along the sides

Use a padded piece of 1×4 wood on a pole (create a "T" shape) as the best tool for gently bumping the inside of the cover

During the blizzard of 1977, when I was working in the greenhouses, one of my colleagues had three of his structures totally buried in snow because of drifting. He dug a hole and tunnelled down to the door and was working inside, buried in snow. That is not recommended today with some of the unpredictable conditions we get!

BEWARE of this sequence which creates a "worst case scenario":

Freezing rain, followed by dropping temperatures, a lot of snow followed by rainfall. It is easy to triple the weight of the snow load in 30 minutes.

From January to April of 2014 there were more structure failures than Norm has seen in all of his 40 years combined. Removing ice and snow is a simple process that could have saved many people a lot of expense. Even with a peaked building, once you have ice on it, snow does not shed as well. Add rain to the package and you can triple the weight in half an hour. Gusts of wind then double that weight.

One other scenario to be aware of:

If your building has come through a major snow event that has been deemed fairly significant, and you feel confident that it survived, please remember: once it has had stress on it, the same amount next time may cause collapse. Make sure that you carefully inspect the building for signs of stress. Even small amounts of perceived stress, can cause significant issues in the future. Being proactive is always easier than being reactive after the fact.

TEMPORARY FIX FOR A LOOSE COVER

There are a number of instances where a cover will need to be installed in less than ideal conditions. This can be either be on a windy day or in the cold (-10C or worse) and the job simply can not wait.

This will almost invariably lead to a situation where the cover will need to be re-tightened on a warmer and/or calmer day.

Doing this temporary fix will get you an extra month of time that you can wait until it warms up and you can do a better job retightening the loose cover.

The lifespan of a cover can very quickly be reduced
if it is repeatedly flapping in the hard wind.

A very effective, temporary fix to give you more time to do the job right, is to put ropes or straps over the building (as in the photos below)

A 1" or 2" wide seat belt type material is ideal but likely you will need to settle for a soft, marine grade rope instead. **Using nylon rope is almost worse then using nothing because of the abrasion factor.**

The idea is to put a strap or rope **between** pairs of hoops every 12' to 16' and pull as tight as you can. Use nails or eye bolts on your base as the spot for securing the ropes or straps.

If your cover is especially loose, it is best to install each of the ropes or straps snugly first. Then go back and tighten them as tight as you can. This will prevent you from pulling too much in one spot.

TIGHTENING A LOOSE COVER

If you need to put the cover on in cooler and less than ideal weather, you will be looking at significant wrinkles once the weather starts to warm up.

You will need to tighten the cover to prevent premature wear due to flapping in the wind.

Tightening does not have to be done all at once. You can do half one day and half on another.

It is important to remember that you are always pulling at 90 degrees to the wrinkles. Most of the tightening will need to be done lengthwise first.

If you have a loose cover and no time this week to tighten things, there is a temporary fix!

- Take a soft length of rope (**do not use nylon!**) and throw it over the building where the cover is particularly loose.

- Tie the rope off at the base as tight as you can.

CHAPTER TWO: BUILDING PERMITS

KEY TAKEAWAY: It is your responsibility to establish what your local rules are prior to installing the structure. You will get farther working with the inspectors than against.

BUILDING PERMITS

A question that we are asked regularly is "Do I need a building permit for this building?" The simple answer is "Generally, yes". The frustrating and unfortunate part is that there seldom is a month where we do not hear a strange interpretation of some rule which we have not heard before. There continues to be a huge variation in the interpretation of the rules. This goes beyond the fact that certain areas get more snow and wind then others and therefore require sturdier buildings. Our focus will continue to be getting an understanding of what it is that you are dealing with so that we can put together a structure package that will serve your needs for years to come. Educating our customers on weather dynamics on these buildings continues to be a valuable component of that process.

Many of our customers, who are putting their new building out of sight and they get along with their neighbours, will put up the building without asking questions. This is certainly not a practice we recommend or encourage but acknowledge as a reaction to officials who do not understand these buildings or how they work. It is difficult to understand why identically fabricated building, installed on nearby locations, can run into a problem simply because of what they are using the building for. Just last week we received calls from two prospective customers, the first had been given a 10-page form to fill out and the other was ready to order his building since he had been specifically told "you do not need a permit for a tent".

In most municipalities, these buildings are classified as low human occupancy, temporary buildings. We have engineer approved drawings for a number of our standard buildings as governed by the Farm Building Code. With the large amount of variations that we offer, we are sometimes in a situation where the building is somewhere between two approved units. It is quite easy for us to upgrade the building to a higher wind or snow rating but that does not mean it will be automatically acceptable without a specific set of engineer evaluated drawings for your site. It is your responsibility to verify these things before building.

CHAPTER THREE: TECHNICAL INFORMATION

KEY TAKEAWAY: Although there are many specific and technical points, it is critical to understand them to have your building succeed

IMPORTANT BASIC ENGINEERING

There are some basic engineering principles which you should be aware of when you are considering some different combinations for your structure. **Knowing the basics will help you stay away from certain pitfalls.**

There are 3 forces on every building which need to be considered if you want it to stay where you put it and in the shape, you built it.

There are

- down force (usually from snow build up)

- up lift (by wind)

- lateral shift (both wind and snow)

Mother nature is not restricted by lack of patience and will work away at any vulnerabilities in the structure, often without notice until it's too late.

When you compare the end profile of a structure to the cross section of an airplane wing, there are similarities. The big difference is that you want an airplane to get off the ground, and you want the structure to stay put.

When an airplane is in the process of landing or taking off, the flaps are extended off the back of the wing to create more surface area and therefore more lift. By building a structure taller, you are sort of doing the same thing, except you want the opposite result.

I had a customer that installed a 30x60 greenhouse on two 12″ steel I beams that weighed three tons each. He thought the structure "wasn't going anywhere". When the wind came over the building, the resulting vacuum on the backside sucked out the back wall. Once the width was expanded to 38′ and the top lowered by 4′, the reduced vacuum caused it to stop moving. This is an example of the airplane wing effect.

There must not be any wiggle room that the weather can work on these vulnerabilities or things will come loose, unstable, and wear out faster.

Security of your building starts with proper anchoring. How much anchoring is enough or too much?

There simply is no such thing as too many anchors. There are also various tips for ensuring that the plastic is tight enough to avoid wrinkling and flapping about, while balancing the issues of it being too tight. This can easily extend the life of your roof cover.

Down force is commonly referred to as snow load. The most commonly asked question is "how is the structure rated for snow load?" Going from wind load to snow load, shape and size do matter.

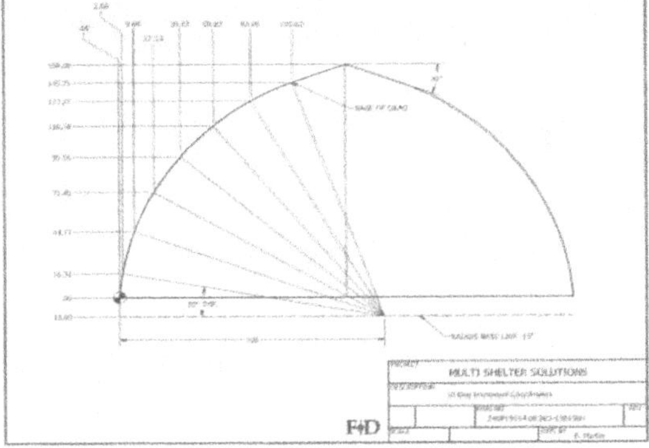

When you are low on the profile of the structure, wind is more of a factor. As you go up the curve, wind is less of an issue and snow is more of the potential problem.

What happens when you go from 20' wide to 30' wide?

50% more width = 100% increase in snow load

50% more height = 100% increase in wind load

How does a structure get evaluated for strength?

Logic would dictate that going 50% bigger would mean 50% stronger or 50% load but it is actually double. Going from 20' wide to 30' wide is an increase of 50%. Because of the magnification rules, the snow load is actually double.

Combine that with the fact that the 30' wide is typically about 50% taller, that also doubles the wind load.

We use rectangular tubing for the hoops of our structures. Even though 1"x3" has 50% more sidewall than the 1"x2", it is actually a little more than twice as strong.

Shape is also a critical factor. 1"x2" rectangular, 1.5" square and 1.5" round can all weigh the same, so they cost the same. However, something with corners is close to 50% stronger.

In engineering terms, the answer depends on where or how your load requirement is. Something round is absolutely the strongest shape for compression. Most of the loads and forces on a structure are not compression loads though. The strength of any shape with corners is magnified. The width of steel contributes to lateral strength, whereas the depth of steel contributes to the vertical strength.

The issue with wider hoops, is that you create more shadows. A 1"x2" hoop spaced 3' apart as compared to 1.5" wide spaced 3' apart represents almost a 5% increase in shadowing. Going to 1"x3" on 4' spacing, is a 25% decrease in shadowing AND it is at least that much stronger.

These numbers will increase or decrease when comparing higher and lower buildings.

How is stability affected when the anchor point is not at the ground?

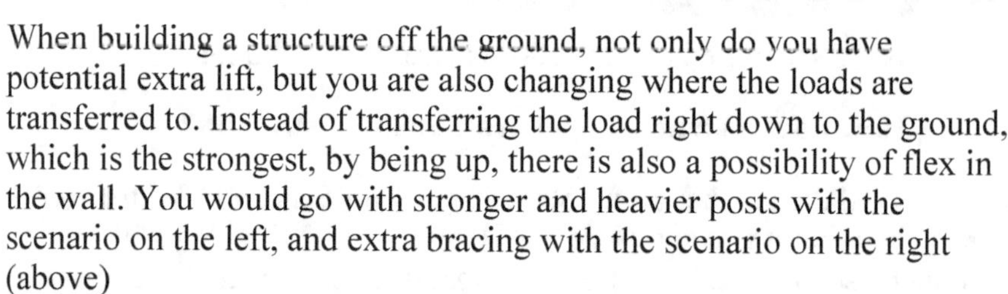

When building a structure off the ground, not only do you have potential extra lift, but you are also changing where the loads are transferred to. Instead of transferring the load right down to the ground, which is the strongest, by being up, there is also a possibility of flex in the wall. You would go with stronger and heavier posts with the scenario on the left, and extra bracing with the scenario on the right (above)

Raising a 15' tall x 30' wide building onto a 4' wall, increases the uplift by 50% but also does some strange things to the lateral forces. Instead of the lateral force being at the ground where it is the strongest, it is up 4' where there is quite a bit more potential for flex. Straight walls catch more wind as well.

What is the minimum space requirement between structures?

Most of the time the question of how much spacing should be between buildings, has to do with snow piling up. Obviously, you need to have adequate space for snow removal equipment in the event that it gets bad.

Consider which way the wind typically comes.

If the wind typically comes across the buildings there will be a significantly uneven snow load on the back side which requires more space. You will be removing snow more often. When the wind is typically coming in line with the building, the snow load is more uniform and requires less space.

Another very important consideration has to do with the shedding of rain. The combination of wider buildings with narrower spaces will require significant enhancement of your drainage capacity.

How does aerodynamics change for multiple units, side by side?

The uplift that is created on the back side of a building does seem to be multiplied when you have multiple buildings. They do not shelter each other; the loads are actually being multiplied.

A customer had a 27x108 building behind a large glass greenhouse and protected at both ends as well. Since the customer perceived it as a protected courtyard, he didn't anchor the base beams. With the wind coming over top of the glass greenhouse and resulting in a vacuum, the structure shifted laterally for 60' before the leading edge caught an obstacle and folded the greenhouse

PART THREE:
IDEAS AND USES

CHAPTER ONE: COMMON APPLICATIONS

KEY TAKEAWAY: There are many versatile uses for these buildings, get creative!

These buildings are great for storing the hay and other equipment for your farm. They can cover your swimming pool to extend your season into late fall/early winter. Park your RV, boat or other fun summer toys over the winter to keep them protected. Plan for a garage so this will be the year you don't need to brush snow off your vehicle.

We have many various applications that our structures are used for, and you will often hear us say the line, "there isn't much we haven't heard in over 40 years of doing this". We have created some standard "packages" as starting points, so feel free to look around and start there to check out what we have to offer. There's always more we can discuss after you've had a look around and discovered a feel for what you have in mind and what we can do for you.

- Large Greenhouses
- Mini Greenhouses
- Hanley Caterpillar Greenhouses
- Movable Structures
- Large Storage Structures
- Small Storage & Garages
- Livestock Shelters
- Swimming Pool Enclosures & Spa Covers
- RV Shelters
- Salt Storage
- Airplane Hangars
- Boat Shelters
- Hunting Shelters
- Loading Docks
- Igloo Round Structures

SWIMMING POOL ENCLOSURE

Installing a greenhouse over a swimming pool is a cost effective and simple way to significantly increase the use of your investment. Even with an unheated pool, you will be extending the swimming time by a minimum of three months. This is accomplished due to the greater heat efficiency which is created by the double plastic cover.

During the swim time, you will have up to 75% decrease in chlorine use and a 75% decrease in sweeping time. The roll up sides will make the temperature comfortable during the day time with adequate ventilation. By closing the roll up sides in the evening you will eliminate the cool evening breezes and control the bugs.

Enjoy swimming without the mosquitoes! The typical package is sold with a double clear cover and a roll up side wall kit. The structure can be fastened directly to your deck or anchored beside the concrete. Consider placing the structure off center to create extra walking/lounging space along one side.

With the wide variety of shapes and sizes available, almost every pool can be covered. The experience can be further enhanced with adding a spa or change house area. A wide variety of ends are available depending on the aesthetics or requirements.

> We had one over our pool as my daughter was growing up and it allowed me to have more time playing in the pool with her because of decreased maintenance time as well as the extended swimming season. It would get up to 96°F sometimes!

RV STORAGE

There are numerous applications where additional headspace takes priority over floor space. The straight wall of the MSS Cathedral shaped structure creates a perfect solution for this situation. This solution is ideal when protecting an RV or trailer. Even though this is our most snow resistant model, the hoops are placed slightly closer than typical due to the wind loads. This shape is the result of simply taking a regular profile arch and reversing what is typically the top and bottom. This is another example of how our innovation creates a "custom" structure at standard pricing. The opaque cover lets in a good level up light while still protecting stored vehicles from fading and other harmful effects.

The simplicity of the required base allows you to keep your options open. A 6x6 (or equivalent) timber pegged to the ground is all that is required. This allows easy relocation if circumstances change. Usually the back wall is framed in with studs and covered with one of our durable covers. The "finishing touch" can be a simple roll up door which allows the whole end to open up. When finishing the ends the should be a small vent near each peak to allow the building to get rid of excess moisture.

It is important to remember that the more often you are in and out of the shelter, the more space you should have around the edges. If you are parking the RV once per year, it is easy enough to be a bit more careful. If you do it frequently, it is probable that one of the times you may miscalculate and run into the shelter.

SALT AND SAND STORAGE

The photo above is our 30' wide put on the ground beside the blocks. You can also mount it on the blocks. Our packages most often come with a tarp cover for both ends. The assembly instructions give pointers on how to frame in the back. The finishing touch is one of our very economical roll up doors which typically keep out 90% of the weather.

These units can easily be mounted onto a beam which is secured to the top of one or more layers of big concrete blocks. It is important to have a seal between the beam and the block so that rain water will run to the outside.

An important area of consideration when mounting a structure to more than two rows of blocks, is the way that the wind load increases exponentially as the height increases. (i.e. 50% increase in height doubles the wind load). This is why we often go with reduced hoop spacing.

Always be aware of the potential outward push of the pile that is being covered.

EQUIPMENT STORAGE

We have a variety of shapes and sizes to suit your equipment storage needs. Our buildings can have very straight sidewalls for more interior space with or without putting it a wall. The recommended covering is a 12-mil woven plastic tarp that is a three-layer white, or green tarp. This will prevent excessive wear and tear on the cover if equipment is bumping into it. The white tarp is more common and what MSS recommends because it lets in light, creating a more usable workspace inside, as well as not absorbing the heat, which creates a longer life expectancy. Both are UV treated to keep the sun from bleaching the contents.

As pictured here, our storage buildings can be set on a knee-wall or posts to give more sidewall and overall height to the structure. Our 30-foot wide building is a great size for hay or equipment storage (other widths available). It has a center height of 15′ and is available in any length that you may need. Our buildings can have very straight sidewalls for more interior space with or without putting it a wall.

Ideal as a carport or for small recreational vehicles, garden furniture or even for a workshop.

LIVESTOCK SHELTERS

Animals thrive in a greenhouse type environment benefiting from

- being dry and out of the wind

- being in the light without being in the direct sun.

- The cushion of air created by the **inflator fan** will <u>reduce the condensation</u>

- **Roll up sides** are added for <u>easy natural ventilation.</u>

Usually customers attach a snow fence or netting to the inside of the arch if the structure is mounted to the ground, so the animals do not come in contact with the cover or run away when the sides are rolled up.

A short wall is also an option to keep the animals away from the plastic while also increasing the sidewall height.

A white tarp covering may be used instead of the double white plastic, especially in situations where the animals are going in and out on their own accord when they require shelter.

LIVESTOCK/GREENHOUSE COMBINATIONS

Plants cannot grow under white plastic. **What if I need this structure to seasonally serve a dual purpose ...part of the year for livestock shelter and part of the year for greenhouse?**

The answer would be different if you were doing winter/greenhouse and summer/livestock then the typical summer/greenhouse and winter/livestock.

Since a greenhouse and a livestock shelter both usually have double plastic and roll up sides, one of the options would be to have the narrow, white plastic on the outside. This means that the roll up sides are only covered with single clear plastic. If you have a high light requirement plant growing in the greenhouse, this will not work. It does work quite well if you are growing more shade tolerant plants.

Another option would be to put a double clear on the structure and then put a third layer of white plastic over the structure for the winter. You can use a thinner, cheaper plastic for this and it would be seen as disposable. Throw it away in the spring. You could also use the better white plastic but you would have to be very careful with removing and folding it in the spring.

Shade cloth is not an option for the winter since it will reduce snow shedding

I remember the first livestock shelter I sold, the customer's vet told him he was crazy and the fluctuating temperatures would cause the animals to die. The customer's logic was that bacteria can't thrive in light and dry and the building was an economical way to keep them out of the weather. Later he told me that the medication savings alone almost paid for the building!

GOLF CART & EQUIPMENT STORAGE

Another application that our structures are being increasingly used for is golf cart storage. These shelters provide golf course superintendents with economical winter protection for the carts and other equipment. During peak season these shelters serve as maintenance areas for equipment and storage for fertilizer. Multi Shelter Buildings are very versatile and the same building can be used for multiple applications. Call today to discuss your requirements and we can help you find just the right structure for your needs.

MARINAS

Help with Shrink Wrapping and keeping the weather off

Our structures have been used by customers such as Hastings Marine and Terry Senecal in Gananoque for large scale protection while shrink wrapping boats and storing boats and RVs. Keep the weather off you and extend the available time for working! These buildings give you the environment to do a more effective job since you won't be affected by wind and moisture.

CHAPTER TWO:

MOVABLE STRUCTURES

> **KEY TAKEAWAY:** There are creative options for season extension once you understand the basic concept of the way the structures work

MOVABLE STRUCTURES

***Please note, we reference greenhouses in this section as it is the most common application for these structures, but they can be used for anything that requires relocating a building**

The idea of a moving structure allows a user, with a little creativity, to protect 2 -3 times as much area with the same building and investment. It is a very simple concept as long as some basic guidelines are adhered to. It can be applied to many of our standard structures.

A significant part of season extension involves **moving an intact structure.** This also applies to storing things in various locations, as well as housing chickens.

This basically allows you to get two (or possibly three) areas of protection from one investment.

For example, we will use the idea of growing crops. The idea is to start a relatively cold tolerant crop very early in the season (the timing will be different in different locations).

1. Once the crop is firmly established in location A, (and it has warmed up) you will move the structure to location B and start another crop.

2. You will harvest the crop in location A and then after working the soil, plant another crop in location A which is intended for fall harvesting.

3. After location B is harvested and before frost you will move the structure back to A.

4. Instead of doing twice in location A you could also choose location C.

A structure can be **equipped with wheels** which will run over the soil. There is quite a bit of flexibility where you go and the terrain you navigate.

The structure can be **equipped with rollers on a track**. This will determine where you go and this is usually intended for moving a bigger structure with fewer people.

The most common method of moving is **sliding the structure on the soil. The base rail can be wood or steel**.

It is critically import to understand the logistics of moving on a structure before you start. It is not hard to move a structure but it is also not hard to do damage.

Having a **plan for proper anchoring** is very important for a moveable structure. <u>Your structure is at a vulnerable state when you release the anchors</u>. Once you start, the job must be completed quickly. You have to be aware that the anchors may not come out or go back in easily so you may need to give yourself some extra time.

One other area of consideration on a moveable structure is the **ends**. There must be some sort of a flap or vent along the bottom so that when a structure is being moved, the ends will not uproot plant material. Generally speaking, to have this ability in the ends takes away from the structural integrity, so some extra anchoring may be required.

The welded rail is $10.90/linear foot. That means if your structure is 36' long, you would calculate 36 x $11 = $396. Our prices exclude installation, foundation, freight & taxes unless otherwise specified. Please inquire with any concerns. *prices subject to change, please contact for current rates

The intent of this is to point out concepts rather than discuss specifics. There are simply too many possibilities to cover them all. It is our purpose here to make sure you realize the possible consequences of some of your ideas and to point out potential pitfalls.

The idea of a moving structure allows a user, with a little creativity, to protect 2 or 3 times as much area with the same building and investment. It is a very simple concept as long as some basic guidelines are adhered to. If these guidelines are not followed, the building can easily sustain significant damage. The stress of pulling must be distributed evenly to eliminate or greatly minimize the risk of damage.

There are many ways you can prepare a building which you want to be able to move. The first question you must ask and answer is "How often and how far do I need to move this?" If once per year you are moving it north the length and once per year you are moving south (scenario #1), you will need to do much less to prepare and stiffen your building then if you are going 500 meters over uneven ground with a 90 degree turn (scenario #2). Most likely you are between the two.

The various choices for a **base** can be as simple as a 4×4 base beam for the small structures or 6×6 for the bigger units. You should never use plain wood in contact for the dirt. Organically certified farms will need to use cedar or metal as your base rail. A metal base rail is also a good idea if the ground is quite wet or when the building is only moved once per year (more likely to stick to the soil with wood). Using multiple, offset layers of wood, your base beam will be one continuous rail which will not come apart with pulling. If you are moving a bigger structure over greater distances or uneven soil, you will be best to consider a 3"x3" structural beam since there is

118

much more strength and durability. If you will be moving your building once per week, you should consider mounting wheels or casters and possibly using a track.

Anchoring your base is another area to give proper consideration. This is not a place to take short cuts. If there are not enough anchors, your building could blow away and if there are too many, it will take longer than necessary to move it. T-posts can easily be used over and over, even in rough conditions. Especially if the T-posts are not too long, they should be used in alternating directions so they work against each other. Screw in anchors, like those on big tents, are very effective but usually require a machine to install and uninstall. Be very careful if you are considering anchoring your building with weights. It usually requires a lot more then you realize. Get a second opinion! If you are going back and forth between the same two spots, you could consider permanent anchors in each location.

The next area of consideration is **ends**. Ends will have to allow the structure to move over uneven terrain since it is rarely smooth. You also have to remember that you will either be moving a structure off of a crop or on to a crop so the bottom of the ends must be able to open up according to the height of crops or obstacles. Your ends will have to be suspended with a movable bottom part cover.

The structure can easily accommodate the weight of the end but you must make provision for the end to be braced. The quantity of vertical end frames will be determined by the width of a building… from 2 for a 12' wide to 6 for a 30' wide.

The other variable is the amount of wind the end will typically be exposed to in your area. End framing can easily be stiffened with long T-posts but you need to remember is that the more that goes into the ground, the more that needs to come out of the ground at moving.

If you need to get in and out with people or equipment while it is sitting in that location, you must build doors of proper size and

location. These doors should be easily removable or have a hinged bottom part. The covering for the bottom part can be as simple as a flap of plastic with dirt on it once the structure is parked. You can also make a horizontal window to flip up for moving and ventilation.

Moving the building is the biggest area of consideration. You need to remember that to get the building moving requires more than double the force then to keep it moving. A very important thing to remember is that unless you have 50% more time available then what you think the job will take … DON'T get started. This is not a job you can complete the next day!

A tractor is the most common equipment for moving the building and typically a tractor has power to spare for this job. **An important thing you have to remember is that you will not likely hear the creaks and groans of stress over the sounds of the tractor until you SEE the stress related damage.** The longer your pulling cables are, the more you minimize this risk.

If you have roll up sidewalls on your building, you should always raise them for moving since this minimizes the risk of the wind getting hold of your building. Especially for your first move… the only good wind is NO wind!

It is important that whatever your structure is sitting on, there should be a "ski" type of extension on the base so that it will not dig into the ground. If you put some cross pieces of steel under the base beam, it will help to break the bond with the soil it is sitting on.

If it is your intention to move this with a V shaped cable attachments from the front corners, you need to remember that you MUST pull on the beam… the arches are simply not strong enough! By pulling with a V, the front of your building will want to narrow and collapse, so a solid cross bar needs to be installed. This cross bar cannot be at ground level since in most situations since it would uproot the crop it is moving over. The ends of the cross beam need to be strong enough so that they can curve down and attach at the beam.

Once you have released your beam from the anchors, you will make that initial pull much less stressful if you go along both sides with a pry bar and every 5' – 8' give it a lift.

As you are moving the structure, the rest of it will want to spread so provision must be made to tie the two sides together. These cross members are usually removable cables with hooks attached. Once again, they should be attached very near to the beam. The higher you need to attach, the more cross cables you will need. Your minimum should be a cable for every 12' of length.

One variation to moving the building with a tractor is to use winches. This allows you to pull on both sides simultaneously and although it is likely to be slower with the tractor, it is potentially much less stressful on the building and it is much easier to react to an impending problem. The best combination would be a winch being held by a tractor if you have to move it more than its own length.

If you are moving a structure often or over longer distances, please call to discuss wheel options.

If your move is scenario #2 (long distance with 90 degree turn), this is going to be more like a 5-point turn. You cannot pull this around a corner without inflicting stresses the structure was not built for.

Structures can also be built low and compact to be more wind resistant. This makes moving simpler so it can be done daily. This is a common practice for free range poultry.

A point I would like to make in conclusion is that although I have never physically moved a structure myself, I have studied stresses on buildings for many years plus I have talked to many people who have moved them.

CHAPTER THREE: UNIQUE AND USEFUL
THINKING OUTSIDE THE BOX

KEY TAKEAWAY: After 45 years, there isn't much Norm hasn't seen, but every once in a while, he must think outside the box and these are the results

THINKING OUTISDE THE BOX

We don't bend any steel before we get an order, so this allows us to provide you a customized shelter, for a standard price! Through more than 30 years' experience creating shelters, we are able to tailor specific solutions for your unique requirements. This page highlights just a few of the times our experience has allowed us to provide customers with the best shelter solution for their application. Call us today with your challenge, and we will be more than happy to find you a shelter solution for your needs!

- Boats

- Igloo Round Structures

- Airplane Hangars

- Hunting Shelters

- Spas

- Loading Docks

- Chicken Coops

- Construction of Apartment Building

- Butterfly Conservatory construction

- and whatever your imagination can conceive!

IGLOO STRUCTURE

We have a unique structure that we have started offering more often. It is a round dome structure, with our standard hoops around a circular ridge piece. We have taken to calling this our "Canadian Igloo" Structure. Plastic is put on in separate pieces so it's not for the new building assembler. We have them being used for everything from seminar areas to storage, whatever you would like a unique application for!

AVAILABLE OPTIONS

- Anchor posts which are hollow steel tubes driven into the ground under each hoop

- Brackets come with each anchor post to attach the base board (nuts and bolts included)

- The heavy duty, galvanized peak bracket comes with the appropriate number of factory welded stubs

- Hoops are rectangular galvanized steel, in one piece from top to bottom

- Cover fastener channel with stainless spring steel inserts

126

 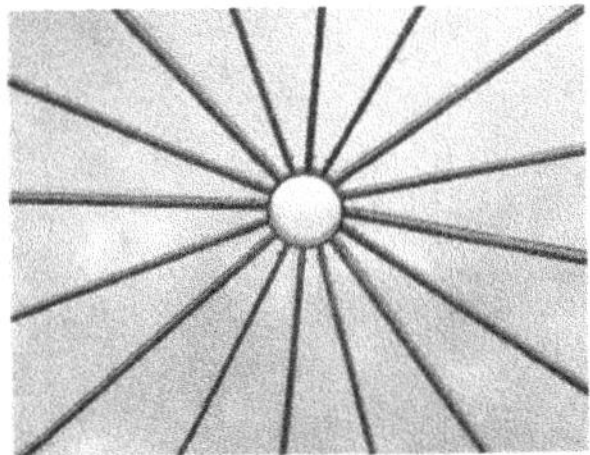

Covering Details

- Igloos typically covered with a single layer of 6mil plastic and have a 5-6 year expected lifespan.

- They can also be covered in a double layer plastic, 12 mil tarp or Lexan polycarbonate

- 6mil clear greenhouse plastic comes with a 4-year warranty against deterioration by the sun.

- White plastic should not be used for plants

I was having a discussion with a customer and he wanted something unusual for his garden center seminars. He asked "Can you do something round?" The challenge was coming up with a center piece. Once I had the idea about a 12" diameter heavy wall pipe, we cut 4" off and welded all the ridge stubs. The customer's sons begged me to get their dad off the hair brained idea, and afterward admitted it wasn't that hard.

AIRPLANE HANGAR

These structures can be customized to accommodate the wingspan of ultralights while still accounting for snow shedding and wind bracing. We have now shipped buildings for this application all over North America!

The challenge encountered when putting a shelter over an aircraft is that the wingspan is often greater than the overall length. Generally speaking, this would require a more expensive structure. When a building is wider, it would also be higher and catch more wind. For ultra-lights and other such light aircraft, one alternative is to make a very low dolly which would allow you to move your craft into the structure sideways.

Since most available buildings are taller than they need to be, the profile can easily be modified to create a little more width. When increasing width, you will decrease the snow shedding ability. This occasionally necessitates reduced hoop spacing.

To start the process of getting a shelter, you will need to know the tip to tip wing measurement and the clearance required. Since most available buildings are taller than they need to be, the profile can easily be modified to create a little more width. **When increasing width, you will decrease the snow shedding ability**. This occasionally necessitates reduced hoop spacing.

Even when the intention is to leave the ends open and allow the air to flow through, it is recommended to close the upper part of the end. This stiffens the building and prevents a significant amount of weather from getting in. Care must be exercised if one end is closed and the other open. One of the other end options is to have a complete end roll up door.

LEAN-TOS

We offer an option of lean-tos for areas where there isn't as much space. Pricing for the lean-tos are generally 60% of the price of the structure. You can see pricing and options on the various application pages and calculate it from there. Please don't hesitate to call us for a firmer price if you have any questions.

All of the Multi Shelter Solutions structures use the 2-part hoop system bolting together in the middle with a continuous ridge. This allows any of our buildings to be used as a lean-to. The size of the lean-to is mostly determined by available wall height where it will be fastened to determine where to look for applicable information double the width of your desired lean-to (e.g. 10' lean-to…look at 20' wide, either regular, high or space saver)

To fasten a lean-to to the wall we can supply individual brackets for the top of each hoop if the support framing is consistent enough (55% cost of full structure) or we can supply a single sided ridge (60% cost of full structure).

One point of extreme caution, you must be aware where snow typically comes off the building where the lean-to is being attached to. One of our "heavy duty" options may be required to provide the required security.

HOUSE BOAT PROJECT

We have also done some unique ones for covering over a boat to live on year-round and lifting to cover the elevator shaft of an apartment building as it was being built

Many times, we get requests for a structure that people will park a boat in. The application above, they wanted a structure to fit ON a 75' converted fishing trawler. The challenge was the sites were not parallel, the top was not flat, and it had two masts! I told him where to measure. He started at the widest and lowest point in increments so he knew how much to cut off the top and bottom of each hoop. In the area of the masts, we supplied a double ridge. He could go sailing down the St. Lawrence with a 20x60, but chooses to just winter in it instead.

THE APARTMENT PROJECT

One of our customers was building a 19-story high rise with an extensive stairwell. This was happening through the winter so protection was required for the block work. They approached me about the possibility of creating a structure that could be removed with a crane. With proper reinforcements and added weight to create stability, the 24x48 building was moved 3x a week to protect the workers and work area. This enabled them to complete one floor a week!

PART FOUR:
WHO WE ARE AND
WHAT WE DO

CHAPTER ONE: PHILOSOPHIES AND VALUES

KEY TAKEAWAY: A family business, we don't sell you a structure, we help you buy one!

Manufacturing & distributing economical shelters for all your growing, housing and storage requirements.

Proudly owned and operated by Norman Eygenraam, this family-oriented business started in the Dundas, Ontario area and has moved up to Palmerston, Ontario for the last 13 years. Specializing in unique shelter construction, we don't bend any steel before we get an order. We sit down with each customer to assess what their structure needs to accomplish and what it is dealing with to help you find the solution that will be most useful for your application. We have many standard variations to offer and aren't afraid to venture outside the box to get the right fit for you!

We don't sell you a structure, we help you buy one!

Norm worked at a nursery operation in his 20s, at a time when cold frames were manually bent steel around a tractor rim. Later he started selling structures with a manufacturer outside Grimsby, Ontario. In 1989, he started on his own, in Dundas Ontario selling greenhouses. As the need for variations arose, his focus turned to manufacturing. In 2005, he moved the operation to Palmerston and became Multi Shelter Solutions. The business focus has changed to include shelters for many more applications.

We bring all that experience to each and every call or email that we receive from potential and existing customers. We feel word of mouth is still the best advertising and strive to give personal attention to every request, from a small hobby shed to multiple large operations.

Our biggest selling point still remains that we don't bend any steel before getting an order, so we are able to customize it to fit in just the right spot or alter how it's done for your unique request. That's how we've come up with our "igloo" structure, the airplane hangars, our "flying" greenhouse that was lifted onto an apartment building, and more! We pride ourselves on being able to help you find your best shelter solution. Sharing knowledge to minimize pitfalls is a key component to educating our customers and creating value for the money.

Multi Shelter Solutions offers an economical alternative with a flexibility that the larger competitors find hard to match. We have worked hard over these years to come up with a balance that provides the economy so many seek, while not sacrificing any quality of the structure or customer service. We can work with you to fit whatever budget you have in mind and publish sample prices freely for you to compare. Feel free to contact us for a custom quote for what you have in mind and we can work together to reach your goals.

With a friendly and helpful staff, we are big enough to serve you, but small enough to care & serve you well. Currently we have 6 employees & growing and are happy to help you with any questions you may have. Conversations often begin with 2 questions

What are you trying to accomplish?

What are you dealing with?

We look forward to your call!

CHAPTER TWO:
GIVING BACK

KEY TAKEAWAY: It is important to Multi Shelters to pay it forward and help make the world a better place

Every year at Multi Shelter Solutions we try to collaborate with non-profit organizations and other volunteer opportunities to provide a shelter at low or no cost.

We have done shelters for Haiti after the earthquake, a shelter for an eye clinic in the Dominican Republic, arches for Magical Lights of Milton that donates back to the Milton Hospital at Christmas, greenhouse to Aroland First Nations in Northern Ontario to provide food for their Native community and learning opportunities for the students, and work with Food Bank projects out on the east coast to help provide fresh, healthy vegetables to those most in need, and the list continues to grow

This is something we believe whole heartedly in and would very much like to work with more causes to help in whatever way we can. We also want to express gratitude for the various opportunities we've had to help out non-profit and not-for-profit groups.

2013 FOODS OF THE FUNDY VALLEY

Ben McMichael is the director of the Moncton, NB area food bank and he has a small greenhouse in his backyard that he uses for teaching and producing food. He approached me at ACORN about supplying a greenhouse for his class. He decided the best candidate for this project was Riverside Consolidated School in the Fundy Valley. The reason I was excited about this and other food bank projects since, is the teaching element, in addition to growing the needed food. We supplied them with a 12x24 greenhouse and it produces food for the kids as well as teaching them to grow it.

It was because of Ben's input that I became aware of a greenhouse for its teaching setting. Upon further investigation, I saw the importance and value of this concept and made the decision to make the donation to the cause, as well as many others.

140

2010 FOTOCAN HAITI SHELTERS

I saw a presentation of the earthquake that happened in Haiti. People were surviving with all sorts of make shift shelters, and I wanted to create something that was more weather resistant that got people off the bare ground. I came up with a 12x12 shelter on a platform and

made a proposal to the director of Friends of the Orphans Canada. He thought it was a fabulous idea and set in motion to do a fundraiser. People could sponsor a structure for $500 which included the structure, cover, base and shipping.

90 structures could fit in one shipping container and with the excitement and momentum created, two full containers were shipped. I was involved in training three individuals who went onsite for assembly in Haiti.

We view a 12x12 building as a shed, and seeing the videos of people moving in with their meagre belongings, they treated it like their personal castle.

2016 AROLAND FIRST NATIONS

I received a call from the principal of the Aroland First Nations School inquiring about a greenhouse options and prices. They were going to receive a grant from Breakfast Club of Canada, which was the organization that was

responsible for feeding most of the kids there every day. Upon hearing of the need of the community and the passion of the principal for teaching the children about food, I decided to donate the balance of the 20x48 greenhouse.

The delivery happened in May 2016 and there was an opportunity to do a presentation to the junior and senior classes and the parents, so I delivered it personally. Sharing in their excitement was definitely an uplifting experience.

MAGICAL LIGHTS OF MILTON

David Geall approached me with his annual project and vision for the new addition. He creates a magnificent themed Christmas light display every year set to music and he wanted a set of arches over his driveway to wrap lights around. Every year hundreds of people come to see David's display, and he raises money for the Milton General Hospital. They have raised nearly $30,000 to date. It's quite the spectacular sight.

If you know of a project that could use our help or are involved with something you'd like to see us put some help behind, please don't hesitate to contact us and let us know about it. This is an ongoing initiative of Multi Shelter Solutions, and as a company, and all our staff, would love to see this continue. Please join us in taking some time to give back and Pay It Forward. A little smile goes a long way.

It is with gratitude that we share this book with you, as well as our first edition: So You Want to Buy a Greenhouse…Your Guide to Planning a Greenhouse Purchase. We hope it helps give you clarity and appreciate your interest in this vast industry.

Photo above courtesy of Aroland First Nations as a special thank you for the greenhouse project. We are grateful to share in their excitement